AF594049

Texas Safari

World Class Big Game Hunting in the State of Texas

published by

The Clear Fork Ranch, Inc.

as a

Guide to hunting big game in the Great State of Texas

Copy No. 1699

A. M. Micallef

Published by Clear Fork Ranch, Inc. Photographs furnished by William Reaves-Lonestar Photography-Austin, TX; Chuck Gordon-Cleburne, TX; and the author, A. M. Micallef. Design and printing by Southwestern ColorGraphics. Distributed by Clear Fork Ranch, Inc., 4800 Bryant Irvin Court, Fort Worth, Texas 76107.

Library of Congress Catalog Card Number 86-071285
International Standard Book Number 0-9616868-0-4

First Edition: June, 1986

10 9 8 7 6 5 4 3 2 1

Printed in the United States of America

Texas Safari

Texas Safari

World Class Big Game
Hunting in the State of
Texas

By

A. M. Micallef

A Guide to hunting Big Game
in the State of Texas

Clear Fork Ranch, Inc.
Fort Worth, Texas

Preface

Writing a book is both a challenge and a lot of fun. Many people helped both with the work and the fun.

First, of course, was my family. Without my wife Janie's patient cooperation and willingness to support my numerous trips and hunts, **TEXAS SAFARI** would not have been possible.

My son, Michael, was a constant hunting companion. Though not yet a teenager, he has become an excellent hunter. Our time hunting together throughout the state of Texas has been a highlight of our relationship, not to mention our hunts in Alaska and Africa.

And my daughters, Amanda and Sarah, were part of the total experience as well. Amanda even joined me on several hunts.

Immediately after I decided to do the book, Nancy Montgomery joined my staff. She has performed innumerable tasks as varied as booking hunts and arranging accommodations to checking the spelling of names, and calling and urging persons to provide some little detail. She took over this task from Sue Stephenson, my Business Administrator, who has continued to help when needed. Later, when Shawn Schack joined my staff, she did the layout of the book and collected the information for the appendix in the back.

Wayne A. Robinson, a freelance writer and friend, joined me on all the hunts. Off and on for 18 months, we hunted together, tape recorded, went over copy, talked to bookstores, wrote letters — the whole nine yards. The result? **TEXAS SAFARI: World Class Big Game Hunting in the State of Texas.** His son, Brett, went along as well and also hunted with Finn Aagaard on the Buttery Ranch.

Additionally, there were some very special people who were extremely encouraging. The Schreiner brothers, Charley Four, Walter and Louie, as well as their father Charley Three, were a constant source of encouragement and help. Fernne Hunt in her capacity as secretary-treasurer of the Exotic Wildlife Association also proved invaluable time and again.

I wanted to write this book because I was so amazed that all these animals were available to hunt in Texas. I knew that my friends in my home state of Michigan, for example, didn't know anything about it. I found out that Texans didn't know either, not to mention those in surrounding states.

Thanks to those mentioned, and those who may have been overlooked, for their invaluable help.

AL MICALLEF
Clear Fork Ranch, Inc.
Fort Worth, Texas

Al Micallef is currently a member of:

SAFARI CLUB INTERNATIONAL

THE NATIONAL RIFLE ASSOCIATION

FOUNDATION FOR NORTH AMERICAN WILD SHEEP

TEXAS AMERICAN TROPHY HUNTERS

DUCKS UNLIMITED

DALLAS SAFARI CLUB

GAME CONSERVATION INTERNATIONAL

EXOTIC WILDLIFE ASSOCIATION

*INTERNATIONAL PROFESSIONAL HUNTERS' ASSOCIATION

TEXAS GAME WARDEN ASSOCIATION

*SOUTH AFRICAN PROFESSIONAL HUNTER'S ASSOCIATION

EAST AFRICAN WILDLIFE SOCIETY

TEXAS WILDLIFE ASSOCIATION

*Honorary memberships

TABLE OF CONTENTS

A. M. Micallef

This is my youngest daughter, Sarah, who was somehow left out of every other picture in the book.

A. M. Micallef

The Clear Fork Ranch is in the business of raising registered Texas Longhorn Cattle. This picture is of Freckles, our prize-winning steer taken in his declining years. Freckles now hangs over our fireplace as a reminder to all of us of the history and heritage of Longhorn Cattle.

CHAPTER I

Discovering Exotic Big Game Hunting In Texas

Like everyone else outside Texas, I at one time told the jokes and made fun of Texas bigness. But once I was here and experienced some of the benefits this state has to offer, I became convinced that Texas has some of the best kept secrets in America. You name it and it's here. If it's not here, it will be — by the gross, of course — and delivered yesterday.

That's Texas. Whatever the task, the goal is always to do it bigger and better than anywhere else. And that's one of the first lessons I learned when our company, Jamak, Inc., moved its headquarters plant to Texas from Detroit, Michigan.

If we had stayed back in Detroit, I wouldn't have believed that a place like Texas existed. Not only has our business prospered, but our Texas employees have a super attitude. They have been the key to our success. Their attitude is identical to that of our neighbors and friends, even the Texas companies we do business with. Whether it's a bank, church or the chamber of commerce, there's an attitude that never says, "Can we do it?" but "Let's do it now before someone else does. And while we're at it, let's do it bigger and better than has ever been done."

Nowhere has that been more true than in the exotic big game industry of Texas. Most of my non-Texas friends can hardly believe there are more varieties of game available for hunting in Texas than in any **nation** in the world! For example, only in Texas are there game ranches that offer one or more of the following animals for hunting:

> Aoudad, axis deer, fallow deer, Catalina goat, blackbuck antelope, sika deer, mouflon sheep, Corsican sheep, Barbados sheep, blesbok, addax, eland, Grant's gazelle, Cretian ibex, Siberian ibex, Persian ibex, Defassa waterbuck, scimitar-horned oryx, Markhor four-horned sheep, sable, Nubian ibex, roan antelope, wildebeest, Armenian red sheep, zebra, Texas ibex, gemsbok, West Caucasian tur, nilgai, barasingha deer, Pere David deer, and Russian boar.

Even some hunters in Texas don't realize that their state is probably the best managed game area anywhere. It would be necessary to travel to a dozen countries and several continents to hunt the same species of animals which can be hunted right here in the Lone Star

State. An added benefit is that it will cost less, possibly be a better specimen, and an equally challenging hunt.

It's always fun to meet people who think big game hunting ended in Africa when the white man was kicked out. Yet had it not been for some enterprising Texans that well could have been true. Disappearing with the hunting would have been several species that would have been extinct except for zoo's. Instead, huge game ranches in Texas are keeping alive both big game hunting and several exotic species of big game.

And it's big like most things Texan. Consider this: the last year hunting was allowed in Kenya (East Africa) was 1978. According to the official records, the total number of animals successfully hunted that year was 6,000. That's a lot of zebra, wildebeest, lion, elephant, rhino and antelope.

And yet, in the single county of Llano, Texas — only one county! — during the hunting season of 1983, 12,000 whitetail deer were successfully hunted. In other words, in one relatively small part of Texas, the hunting of one species was double all the hunting during a full year in Kenya, a nation which many regard as having been one of the best places to hunt in the world.

I first learned about the exotic big game available in Texas while on a whitetail deer hunt at the famous YO Ranch in Mountain Home, Texas. After two or three trips, it began to dawn on me that there were some strange animals on that ranch and they weren't cattle or whitetail deer either. When I inquired about them, I learned that they were part of a long time exotic big game breeding and management program that began in South Texas during the 1930's.

Now 50 years later there are scores of game ranches that have a variety of big game hunting available. Some, like the YO, have thousands of acres of land set aside for hunting the finest exotics in the world.

Once I had bagged my first exotic big game, I was hooked. Hunting a beautiful blackbuck antelope, or a fallow deer, an aoudad sheep, or scimitar-horned oryx are experiences I never thought I would have. That they would take place in Texas was even more unlikely. But such experiences take place daily; and for me they're unlike any other hunting experience I've ever had.

I was so impressed with the challenge they offered, that I decided to dig deeper and to learn more about the ranches and the game that are available. But when I searched for literature and books on the subject I was amazed to discover there is very little. The more I looked, the less I discovered.

That's when I decided that publishing a book on hunting exotic big game in Texas was an opportunity for which I was ready. I had never written a book before, but I was an avid hunter, and I was confident that with help I could produce a book that would provide useful information for hunters.

What I've tried to do is introduce the hunting enthusiast to exotic big game hunting in Texas. To do that I've described some of the best big game ranches and the type of hunting experiences they offer. Each is unique. They vary in cost and challenge. They have different animals available and different facilities. But each is a real challenge.

I've personally hunted all the ranches I've written about. And I've recounted as accurately as I know how the hunting experiences they offer.

Additionally, I've described the kind of animals that are available for hunting and provided pictures of them. With that I've offered my evaluation of the kind of hunting they present.

But no book can really create the fun and excitement of this rarest of hunting experiences. Hopefully though, this will be an invitation for you to try it, to learn about it, and to enjoy it. That's my hope and wish.

William Reaves, Lonestar Photography

Mature axis male. One of the most beautiful exotic deer in Texas. A personal favorite of mine.

CHAPTER II

The YO:

when only the best is good enough.

When I think of the YO, I think of **big**: 100 square miles of land, and the largest private hunting area of its kind in the world. It's not only big, it has one of the finest hunting programs in the state. And it's based on sound management and good business practices. Equally important, it's rooted in more than 100 years of Texas history. When people talk about Texas, the YO is the symbol of what they mean.

In its heyday, it comprised 550 thousand acres from which they drove more than 300 thousand Longhorns along the Western Trail to Dodge City. In fact, I was first introduced to the YO due to my interest in Longhorn cattle. As you would expect, the YO has the largest herd of registered Texas Longhorns in the world and is one of the nation's leaders in the development and support of Longhorn cattle raising.

Charles Schreiner, III, known to everyone as "Charley Three," first began the re-introduction of Longhorns to the YO in the 1950's with the purchase of six calves — one bull and five heifers — from the Wichita Mountains Wildlife Refuge in Lawton, Oklahoma. His enthusiasm for the breed was a primary force in the creation of the Texas Longhorn Breeders Association. And the care for pedigree which he insisted was instrumental in establishing the W. R. (Wildlife Refuge) bloodline as one of the best of the breed.

And as an early attention getting incentive for the breed, he recreated a modern-day Longhorn trail drive from San Antonio, Texas, to Dodge City, Kansas, complete with cattle, cowboys, Indians, and a sheriff's posse.

My first trip to the YO was for one of their Longhorn cattle sales and round-ups. While there, I saw more whitetail deer than I'd ever seen in my life. I inquired about hunting them and soon had a reservation made. Surprisingly, I have no recollection of seeing any of the thousands of exotic animals at the YO. I guess whatever wild game I saw, I assumed it was a whitetail of some variety or other.

Too, I had the impression from the media that most of the big game of the world was in danger of extinction. If someone had told me I could hunt exotic big game in Texas, I'm not sure I would have believed them. It would have been equally difficult to believe that there were hundreds of thousands of exotic big game in Texas and that big game ranches like the YO are the key to the survival of several of the species.

When I went back for my whitetail deer hunt with a good friend, Jim Hancock, I learned about the superb variety of exotic big game available. There were black-buck antelope from West Pakistan, sika deer from Japan, Taiwan, and Manchuria, fallow deer from England, axis deer from India, the elusive aoudad mountain sheep from North Africa, the mouflon sheep from the Grecian Islands, a specially bred Ibex from Europe and Central Asia, as well as scimitar-horned oryx and eland from Africa. And as part of their game conservation program, I also saw zebra, giraffe, ostrich, emus, addax, barasingha, buffalo, elk, gazelle, gnu, impala and rhea. The more I saw, the more interested I became.

Now, after a couple of dozen exotic big game hunts on the YO, I'm convinced it offers almost any type of hunting a person could want. It's possible to fly in for an afternoon, hunt for five hours, and jump back on a plane all in the same day. The meat will be dressed, and the antlers or horns taken to the taxidermist for mounting. And if the hunt was not successful, there's no charge for anything more than food and the time of the guide and hunt. However, not to spend more time would be a mistake; two days should be the minimum. Getting to know the Schreiners — Charley Four, Louis and Walter — or staying at the YO Hilton in Kerrville or eating in The Chuck Wagon at the ranch are all an integral part of hunting at the YO.

That's when the variety of hunting options at the YO become available. They can accommodate those who want to hunt on horseback or "safari style" in trucks or vehicles. Naturally, fair chase hunting on foot is always an option.

Due to the size of the YO, a combination of on foot and safari style is probably the most feasible. And for native game, such as wild turkey and whitetail deer, there are ample blinds available.

Once into exotic big game hunting, you will find the YO is also a place for record-book animals. The YO has great game quality. The combination of the outside leases they manage, along with the game available at the headquarters ranch, provides probably the best game overall in the state. That doesn't mean a particular ranch might not have a slightly better stock of one specific animal. But any animal hunted at the YO will be of the highest quality.

Super accommodations, terrific support systems, and great food, all in the setting of a story book atmosphere: that's the YO. It's a hunting experience that should not be missed. Here were some of the best:

A.M. Micallef

Magnificent record book chocolate-brown fallow, in velvet.

HUNTING FALLOW DEER AT THE YO

Hunting any kind of animal at the YO can be a tremendous challenge. Like most things, it usually depends on how much time and energy are invested. One of the most fun hunts I've had at the YO was a fallow deer hunt in the fall.

I had returned three days earlier than anticipated from hunting Kodiak bear in Alaska. I'd taken a nine-foot bear my very first day out. Since I'd already slotted the days for hunting, rather than going back to work I grabbed a half night's sleep, picked up my son, Michael, and headed for the YO.

It so happened that we had chosen the very best time to hunt fallow deer — early October. That's when their antlers are out of velvet and they haven't had enough time to start breaking them off by fighting over does.

Too, fallows have some of the most impressive racks of any animal. Their palmated antlers —like a Moose's — are beautiful.

I had requested Uncle Warren as my guide for this particular hunt. We were looking for a record-book fallow deer. Uncle Warren reported that he had spotted a big white fallow a week or two earlier. We loaded up in his ranch wagon and headed for the range in which he had made the initial sighting. Once there, we began to travel safari style across several thousand acres until we located what appeared to be some fallow deer.

We stopped about 300 yards out and carefully moved around so that the wind was in our face. Then we inched up over a rise and put the glasses to them. There were five or six does with one big white buck. It was their annual mating season and the buck was in rut. He was moving around so much that I couldn't get a good shot. Finally, I told Uncle Warren that I was going to try to get him before he headed into the brush. He agreed it was worth a try. I snapped a shot off just before the buck disappeared into the brush. I missed him completely. We spent the rest of the morning and afternoon looking for him or something that would compare to him, but with no luck.

Toward evening, about a half mile ahead of us, we glassed what looked like a big brown fallow lying under a tree. I decided to give up on the white fallow and go for this one.

The wind was to our back so we spent an hour or more glassing him. When we were no more than 150 yards away he was spooked by the flight of a blackbuck antelope we had jumped. The fallow ran off about 200 yards away from us, then stopped and turned towards us. He was a good 350 yards away, but with just enough clearing so that I felt sure I could get him. I scoped him in, allowing for the long distance, and squeezed off a shot. My bullet hit him in the front chest cavity and went through the top part of the heart. He leaped and fell on the spot. He was a prize trophy and scored great in the Burkett Trophy Record Book.

THE WHITE FALLOW DEER THAT KEPT GETTING AWAY

But I still wanted a trophy white fallow. With the animal population at the YO, I was confident there were others; finding them was the key.

Toward the middle of the afternoon we finally spotted a big white buck on top of a hill. I slipped out of the ranch wagon and inched forward about 200 yards. When I stopped I was less than 125 yards away.

I took aim... and missed! Uncle Warren said I hit a branch. I didn't see a branch at all. But branch or not, I missed him completely. There was a rocky ledge behind him and I didn't even see any dust from the impact of the bullet on the rock.

He ran and we followed him up the hill on to the top of

a flat mesa. We walked around for about an hour and periodically caught glimpses of him but never enough to get a clean shot.

We finally gave up and circled back to where we had killed the brown fallow the previous day. There was what looked like another white fallow in the same area. He had a good rack on him, so I decided to take him.

Unfortunately, he was lying down next to a doe. I could get a clean shot on his neck and about a third of the top of his shoulder. I don't know what possessed me but instead of shooting him in the neck I hit him in the top half of the shoulder. That was too high, but nonetheless, he fell over on the spot. I proceeded to walk up to him to measure his antlers. I was only a few feet away, when he jumped up and started running.

That was a good lesson to learn: when shooting an animal, if it's not a good clean shot, either wait until he's down for good or squeeze off an insurance round. (Last year in Alaska in the same area in which I was hunting, a hunter thought he had made a kill shot on a big brown bear. After about ten minutes he walked over and poked his knife in the bear to start skinning it. The bear reared up and slapped him with a paw that killed the man on the spot!) If a wild animal is not down for good, walking up will shock him even more. It's amazing what adrenalin they can draw on when frightened, even though they may be mortally wounded.

Unfortunately, I hadn't waited and off the deer went. As with every hunting ranch I know anything about, a wounded animal has to be found. Even though it would soon be dusk, we followed him on foot. He felt our pres-

A. M. Micallef

White fallow, taken at dusk on the YO Ranch.

sure which meant he was less likely to stop, but we had no other alternative than to stay with him. Consequently, I had to take some high risk shots while he was moving. I couldn't seem to get a good one. I broke a leg one time, and shot him in the left rear quarter another. Still, he kept on going.

We realized later that he was making a giant circle right back to where we began. About ten yards from my first shot, we spotted him starting up the hill again. This time I took very careful aim. I hit him in the neck bone and he fell immediately.

When we started dressing him, Uncle Warren mentioned that he had already started to stiffen up as though he'd been dead for 30 minutes or more. Evidently, adrenalin was all that kept him going. He had taught me a lesson I'd not soon forget.

A KILL ON UNCLE WARREN'S PICKUP

One of the most memorable hunts I've ever had at the YO, had nothing to do with an animal but with one of the YO's guides extraordinaire, Warren Klein, or Uncle Warren, as he's known to everyone.

Uncle Warren is what you like to think of when you envision the kind of men who made Texas great. He's tall, raw-boned, and rugged. Self-made, owner of land worth seven figures, and yet he works each day as though he had to. With his wife of 52 years, Cordelia, he lives a simple unpretentious life, enjoys his Red Man tobacco, and at 78 can still put in a full day's work with the best.

Part of his ranch land forms the entryway to the YO. Most people probably think it's part of the YO. That seems to be okay with Uncle Warren for he's been a part of the YO so long that he seems like one of the family. For certain, the Schreiners treat him with the affection of a family member.

One day after we'd hunted and killed a super sika deer we were driving through a game range of about 5,000 acres when we kept smelling something burning. Since we were in Uncle Warren's pickup, I didn't do much more than call his attention to it. I had learned that Uncle Warren didn't have a great respect for automobiles. (I don't think he had forgiven them for replacing the horse!)

As we were riding through the pasture, my son, Michael, who was sitting in the front seat, shouted, "The car is on fire!" I leaned forward from the back seat and bent my head as low as his, and sure enough there was a blaze coming through the fire wall. Evidently, the odor we had smelled must have been transmission or brake fluid spraying on the block and it had caught the engine on fire.

Uncle Warren stopped in disgust, and while I rushed around unloading our gear, he calmly started searching for the case of Red Man Tobacco he always kept handy. (He kept at least 10 or 12 packages available.) He found it while I took his gun, binoculars and everything else out. He seemed unaware there was anything he should worry about other than his next chew. Michael and I hurried out of range 100 yards or so and kept looking back at the truck which had turned into an inferno. We expected the gas tank to blow any second.

But what I couldn't believe: all the time we were running and turning around and exclaiming at the magnitude of the fire, Uncle Warren was striding toward the ranch headquarters, never once looking back. When Michael and I would describe how big the fire was, Uncle Warren would spit and keep walking. In fact, he didn't see the truck again until three weeks later when he had to take the insurance adjuster out to see it!

When we returned to The Chuck Wagon and I told the Schreiners about the fire and Uncle Warren's response to the truck, it almost stopped the operations of the ranch for the rest of the day. Louie's comment was that he was surprised Uncle Warren hadn't put a bullet in it!

Uncle Warren — he's one of a kind.

A. M. Micallef

Record book sika taken from the YO Ranch. Taken with my son, Michael and good friend, Tom Ralf.

THE ORIENT'S MOST BEAUTIFUL EXPORT: SIKA DEER

Sika deer are beautiful animals. Though small bodied, they have a striking head and antlers. When frightened, they make a sound almost like a barking dog.

Tom Ralf, a hunting friend of mine from Ft. Worth, and my son, Michael, and I went with Uncle Warren on a sika deer hunt. I had made it clear that I wanted record-book quality if possible. Uncle Warren agreed to try to help us find one.

We hadn't been out for long until we caught a glimpse of one, just before it disappeared into a heavy growth of live oaks.

We spent the rest of the afternoon tracking him without any luck. We were about ready to give up, when we came around a large growth of live oaks. There he was, not more than 50 yards away.

It's ironic, but having a powerful scope when that close can be a real drawback. Uncle Warren had always told me that in hunting, the magnification on the scope should not be set any higher than four or five, even though mine was an excellent scope with a range from three to nine.

When I asked him why, he said that anything higher than a five so distorts the closeness of the animal that it makes an accurate shot very difficult. On a nine, for example, the animal will look close enough to touch. He said that one of the reasons animals are missed so many times when at close range is because the scope makes the target look so big. The target needs to be small enough so the animal can be made out plainly and aim can be taken very carefully.

He also said that kind of preparation is an incentive to help control the movement of the rifle as well. With too strong a power, it's easy to be deluded into thinking that a little movement doesn't matter: after all, see how close the game is! But a one-quarter inch movement can mean completely, missing or else only wounding the animal.

I knew that from other hunting experiences. A month before this hunt, when backing up another hunter on a bear hunt, I had my scope set on nine. As the bear came running toward me, he was so big in the scope that I fired too quickly and moved the rifle. I either missed him completely or else hit him in the foot.

This time though, I had my scope set on four. Any more, and I wouldn't have had a shot. But he was still so close that when I sighted him in, the only thing I could see was his chest. I squeezed off the shot and the sika dropped immediately. My bullet had gone right through the heart.

When it was measured for the record book, it was in the top four. To this day I haven't seen a bigger or better one.

Chuck Gordon

Trophy Mouflon

THE MOUFLONS OF CORSICA

Shortly before Christmas, I decided to schedule a wild sheep hunt at the YO. I had been intrigued with the beautiful horns of the mouflon, which is a wild sheep from Corsica. I talked with Walter Schreiner, arranged for Uncle Warren to guide, and soon had the plans in place.

Because mouflon tend to bunch, they're sometimes not the most challenging hunt. However, Uncle Warren told me that on one of the larger 5,000 acre areas he had seen two old rams that had incredible spreads on them. He felt certain they could be record book.

We drove to the range and stopped to ask a couple of the ranch hands if they had noticed the rams in any of the ranges. They said they had seen some several weeks previously, but had no idea where they were now.

We spent the next several hours combing the range, both in the range wagon and on foot. It was tough sledding with several mesas that we had to climb. There were some enormous boulders and high rocky areas. Naturally, there were hundreds of scrub oaks, much underbrush and flat ground.

We spent the afternoon walking and glassing, riding and glassing. Finally around four in the afternoon, we saw two good-sized rams at the base of a mesa. Uncle Warren said they looked like the two we were after. They were a half mile or more away. I glassed them, and not being real experienced, I didn't know whether or not they were outstanding. Uncle Warren left it up to me to decide whether I wanted to take them or not. I decided I wanted to look around more so we decided to keep looking.

We found several smaller animals but none that matched the two we had seen earlier. Our job now was to find them again.

We drove for another hour with little luck. Worse, we were close to the winter solstice — the shortest day of the year — which explained why we had hardly half an hour's worth of daylight left.

I felt like I'd climbed every mesa on the ranch, but Uncle Warren felt they might be back at the same mesa we'd seen them near earlier. We drove over to the base of it again and looked around, but didn't see them. Uncle Warren said it was possible they had worked their way up the trail and to the top of the hill.

He said if I wanted to get them before dark, I better climb up there. So I proceeded to stumble my way through the rocks, scrub oaks, and underbrush of a YO mesa.

When I reached the top of the hill, I looked over the edge. Sure enough, about 200 yards away, in a clearing no more than 100 yards wide filled with a bunch of scrub oak and cedar, were the two rams we had been searching for.

They were grazing near one of the scrub oaks, with the larger of the two on the inside. Fortunately, he was standing about a foot ahead of the other one. After an afternoon's comparison, I could tell they were both excellent mouflon.

I realized this time that I had better take one while I had the chance. If they moved, there would be no way to find them again on this day.

Too, as dark as it was, if I only wounded him we'd have a heck of a time ever finding him. The ground cover was as dense as it can come. It looked like some dwarf jungle.

I lay on a flat rock and raised the gun. I needed to break both shoulders to keep him from running at all. Uncle Warren had crawled up beside me. He nodded when he saw what I was going for.

I squeezed off a shot and he dropped. By the time we walked up to him, he was dead. He had a great set of horns. It had been a great hunt!

A. M. Micallef

Uncle Warren with axis I'd taken on the YO Ranch, still in velvet. The excitement of the moment got to me, this axis had another 5 to 10 inches growth!

THE MOST BEAUTIFUL OF THE TEXOTICS: THE AXIS

Of all the exotic big game in Texas — and there are now more than 50 species — the axis is my favorite. The meat is excellent eating, the animal has a beautiful coat, and the antlers on a big axis can be spectacular.

Even when hunting for other game, it's hard to pass up a good axis. That happened to me most recently while hunting at the YO with Jim Van Hook, a friend and customer from Ford Motor Company. My recommendation had been that he go for an axis. Uncle Warren helped us find a beauty. Jim was as elated, as I was for him.

The next morning, we had some extra time and went out more for sightseeing than anything. We talked about the possibility of taking a sika if we saw a big one, but I had no serious hunting intentions.

It was a beautiful Spring morning. The grass was green, the trees fully leafed, and wild flowers blooming everywhere. It was like a giant park.

We had been driving for a couple of hours when we approached a large clump of live oaks. About 175 yards away in a creek bottom, stood an axis buck with a huge body and what looked to be an incredibly large set of antlers.

I had no intentions of taking another axis. But this axis was in velvet which made his antlers appear twice as large. They hardly came out of his head before they went straight left and right. Then they curved into a marvelous arc.

For a millisecond, I debated whether to take another axis. I already had a record-book one, but I couldn't resist. I stepped out of the ranch wagon and quietly inched forward for the next 20 minutes. Still I couldn't get a clean shot. The river bottom was filled with all kinds of trees.

I took my time. Finally, I maneuvered into position and made a clean shot on him. He fell in his tracks.

He was as big on the ground as he had been from the wagon — no "ground shrink" this time. He finished in the record book and would have gone higher had not there been a penalty for his being in velvet. Another six to ten weeks and he would probably have had the biggest axis antlers I'd ever seen. As big as they were now, they still stopped about three-quarters of the way up. The tips were blunt without any point yet on the top. I had taken him too early. He would have been one incredible record book animal if I had waited. But, he made one beautiful trophy.

William Reaves, Lonestar Photography

Two magnificent aoudads, the most challenging exotics to hunt in Texas.

CHAPTER III

Triple C Ranch:

a matter of inches — trophy aoudads.

One of the things which excites most long-time hunters is the possibility of bagging a true trophy animal. Whatever the species, knowing that it is one of the biggest of its kind makes for a rare hunting experience. And if the trophy is also one of the most difficult of hunts, that makes it even more worthwhile.

That's why I was raring to go when I learned about the possibility of an aoudad sheep hunt on a game ranch leased by the YO that had not been hunted for 20 years. I was told that the director of the Ft. Worth Zoo had stocked the area with aoudad and simply left them alone. Only in the past year had hunting been introduced. In fact, it was such a rich reserve that its **average** animals had horns that far exceeded the 26 inch record-book level of all of Africa!

Joining me on the hunt would be two members of the famous Schreiner family, Louis and Walter. They were both excellent hunters, and Walter is a world class hunter.

The location was the Triple C ranch, located in some of the most picturesque parts of central Texas, and less than 75 miles from Ft. Worth near Glenrose. But the nearness of the Metroplex should not be misleading. The terrain is rugged hills, trees, arroyos, draws, and more than enough cover to hide the most elusive of big game mountain sheep.

We drove to Glenrose on a Thursday night, and were met by Louie and Walter for the drive to the ranch. Carroll Curry, the owner met us in time for a quick drive of the perimeters of the ranch.

We went back to the lodge, where the steaks the Schreiners had brought were charbroiling. They were the biggest and best I'd had in a long time. Soon afterwards we hit the hay to be ready at the crack of dawn for the hunt.

At 5:30 we hit the floor. We debated momentarily whether to eat breakfast, or to take Carroll's suggestion that we scan the area and then come back to eat. We decided to look first — a big mistake since we didn't get back for breakfast until after noon!

It was still dark when we parked our trucks and began the search for trophy aoudads (horns of at least 30 inches or more). By the time we had walked a half hour or more we topped a hill overlooking a tree-filled draw. Slowly, we began to scan the opposite hillside. Even though it was past 7:00 p.m., we needed more sunlight.

Walter made the first sighting. Across the draw, on the opposite hill were several aoudad. How many was difficult to say because they blended so beautifully into the hillside. But as they moved and milled around, we realized there had to be a bunch of them.

Normally, that's great news for a hunter. But with aoudads, it can be a liability. Their size, coloring, horns and coat are so similar that it's almost impossible to tell any difference between them from a distance. In fact, there are times when simply picking ewes from rams is no small task given some of the underbrush and distances. The only clue is that most of the really older rams darken slightly.

While it was great to spot a herd, the fun was just beginning. In those 40 or more sets of horns, on animals that all looked alike, was there a record-book set?

In addition to their look-alikeness, the other most difficult part of hunting aoudads is the inability to get close to them. We were at least 500 yards away (that's the length of five football fields), trying to pick out a trophy ram which might have horns only an inch or two longer than ten others surrounding him.

Their ability to see for a mile or more, their keen smell and hearing, make it almost impossible to keep them in one place long. Knowing this we froze as we tried to glass the herd for a prize. But within seconds, they were alerted, pulling up, staring, and starting to mill.

There was one buck that stood out. His horns were far superior to any of the three aoudads I had hunted successfully before. But he was halfway behind a large cedar that made it next to impossible to be certain he was the animal I wanted. Then too, it was early in the morning, and we had hardly been out at all. Did I want to make a kill before the day was even begun?

I talked with the Schreiners, and we agreed that this would probably be one of the biggest I would see. From where we were, his horns looked to be 30 inches or more, which was my goal on this hunt.

If my shot were not a kill shot, it would take 15 minutes or more to go down the hill, cross the draw and climb up the next hill. By then, if I had only wounded him, he would be next to impossible to find.

As we waited, the herd began to break away. But the one I had sighted moved out only a foot or more from the cedar. I decided to take him.

I finished glassing and changed to the scope on my .270. The base on his horns was enormous, and the length looked to be much larger than the others in the herd.

How far away was he? The steep hill, the draw between us, and the hill they were on, made it difficult to judge. Louie and Walter felt it was somewhere between 400 to 500 yards. That would mean the bullet would drop as much as 18 inches from where I would aim.

I decided to shoot for the heart, behind and low on his right front shoulder. I sighted where I wanted the bullet

A. M. Micallef

Twenty-nine and a half inch record book aoudad taken at the Triple C with Schreiner brothers, Louis and Walter.

to penetrate, then raised my aim about 18 inches — at the thin air.

When I squeezed the trigger, the shell exploded in the draw like a cannon. The hillside seemed to shift, as aoudads fled from places we hadn't even seen them.

And my aoudad? I couldn't see him anywhere. The distance, the blurring of fleeing sheep, and the thick underbrush and coverage made it impossible to know if I had wounded, killed, or missed.

We readied to go down the hillside. The ground cover was so thick and looked so much the same, that Louie stayed back on top of the hill to give us directions. We slowly picked our way through the scrub oaks, rocks, cedars and hills; then across a draw and up the hill.

When we neared what we thought was the area, we broke into a clearing to have Louie direct us. He yelled us to the spot. There lay my trophy aoudad, behind the tree where I had first sighted him. It had been an instant kill.

Now began the task of cleaning and moving him to where we could haul him in. Despite a harsh winter, he was full and heavy. Walter counted the rings on his horns and estimated him to be nine to ten years old.

We pulled out the tape measure. I knew he was bigger than anything I had ever shot, but was he 30 inches? Tough luck, his horns were twenty-nine inches long one-inch short of my goal, but at least three inches longer than any I had ever shot before and a record book entry for certain.

Now came another difficult decision for me: should I keep hunting until I found a 30-incher? Obviously, they were there and Carroll assured us there was even a 34-incher. But could we find them in one day?

I wanted one bad and Louie did also. We decided to keep on hunting — to heck with breakfast.

My shot had really announced the hunt, which meant the pressure was going to be felt by the rest of the aoudads. Finding the big one would be even tougher.

We walked back to our truck and visited with Carroll. He told us what the options were, and where the most likely locations would be. Then he pointed us to a steep hill topped by a huge boulder. "Get up on that rock and wait. I guarantee you'll get a great shot before the day's out."

His advice seemed sound. We split up. The Schreiners headed one way, and I headed for the big rock. What would happen in the next hours was a comedy of errors which we would never have believed could happen.

As I sat on the rock, I saw a new herd come trotting by. They were nervous and milling around, weaving in and out of the bushes and cedars. Then I saw one: record book all the way. A massive set of horns, a dark coat, and trophy book for sure.

I waited for a moment to see if they were going to settle down, but they were spooked. The more I waited, the less was the likelihood of their staying put.

When I was positive he was the big one I wanted, I decided to go for it. I put my glasses down, and tried to locate him in my scope. They were restless, and my trophy shot had moved behind a cedar. Just as I started to go to my glasses again, he stepped out from behind the cedar and turned facing me — or so I thought. He was not more than 200 yards away. I drew a bead on his heart and squeezed the trigger. He made a spectacular leap in the air and then fell right on his head.

For a second, as the other aoudads began fleeing, I thought I saw another ram with a larger set of horns. Louie would like him I knew. Off the big rock I went. But when I reached my kill I immediately had a sick feeling in the pit of my stomach. Though he was not trophy class, he had an enormous base on his horns. But in length, it was doubtful if his horns were more than 26 inches.

I couldn't believe it. That meant the old ram I had seen running away must have stayed behind the cedar, and because of the base on this one, I had mistaken him for the one I had glassed.

Just then I heard Louie's rifle go off twice. **He shot my ram** I told myself. They wouldn't believe that I had killed the animal in front of me. I already had three just like him. I measured him and he was 26½ inches. **Great, in Africa, but not for Texas.**

What was done was done. In a little while, Joe, the ranch foreman found me and we began cleaning my kill. Then I heard Louie's rifle go off again. "They must have had to chase him down," I said to Joe. He grinned and I mumbled to myself that I should have gotten him.

Just then there was a noise in the bush and I looked up and saw a ram acting strangely, almost heading straight for us. He had to be wounded. I wiped the blood off my hands, grabbed my rifle and finished him off.

When Joe and I walked over to him, we saw that Louie had evidently made a gut shot and a leg shot. His third shot must have totally missed. And I could tell without measuring that his horns were going to be big — probably bigger than mine.

I felt confident they were still trying to find this aoudad. Not only did I want to let them know where their kill was, I was not above ribbing them about my having to finish off their shot for them. While Joe finished dressing mine, I went to look for Walter and Louie.

A quarter of a mile or so away, I saw them. When I got close enough, I yelled that I had their aoudad. I was totally unprepared for their reaction. I thought what I had to say would be great news — they wouldn't have to stalk a wounded animal through that incredible underbrush. But it stunned them. Walter said, "What do you mean you have our aoudad?"

When I got closer, I saw why he asked. They were skinning another aoudad. My first thought was that Walter had decided to take one too. Not the case. It took some time, but we finally determined what had happened.

It seemed that Louie had indeed shot the wounded aoudad which I had finished off. He had tried a running shot and hit the gut. He quickly squeezed off another round but the animal raced away with the rest of the

A. M. Micallef

Al (left), Louis Schreiner (right), and four trophy aoudads who could be close relatives of ours. (Notice the nose similarities!)

herd. Walter and Louie gave chase until Walter saw a limping aoudad that was not keeping up with the rest of the fleeing herd. That had to be the wounded ram, they thought, so Walter took Louie's rifle and fired quickly, dropping the ram in its tracks. It had taken three shots but they got him — or so they thought.

Then I arrived to explain that a wounded ram had almost walked into me, and that he had been shot twice, once in the gut and another in the back leg. Walter and Louie both swore that when Walter took his last shot it was at a wounded ram that was limping real bad.

Then Louie happened to notice the feet of the ram they were dressing. They were badly deformed with one of its hooves turned way under. That explained why he was limping and why he was running slower than the rest. It also meant in the space of one morning, we had two aoudads we didn't want.

An expensive set of mistakes, but probably more fun than any hunt I'd been on with the Schreiners. The comedy of errors in our shots was something we would never have believed beforehand. But that's the challenge of hunting aoudads — even when you find them and get a shot, you're never sure. Though I was disappointed, in reality all four animals were quality of the highest sort, even if they weren't the 30-incher's we were looking for. There would be other hunts and other chances for trophy aoudads — the Triple C would be the place to try again.

William Reaves, Lonestar Photography

Magnificent barrel-horned axis.

CHAPTER IV

Onion Creek Ranch:

where the deer and the antelope play.

Though the 55,000 acre spread of the YO Ranch in Mountain Home provides some unique and challenging hunting experiences, it's indicative of the Schreiners to want to offer more. To do that they've leased some of the best hunting acreage in Texas and added it to their hunting program.

And none is finer than the famous Onion Creek Lodge, 30 miles south of Austin, Texas. Its thousands of secluded, rolling acres create a true hunter's paradise. In addition to the exotic game stocked, it has some of the finest whitetail deer and quail hunting in Texas. In fact, owner J.C. Ruby built a private whitetail deer blind on the ranch for his friend, the late president from Texas, Lyndon B. Johnson.

But what I was interested in was its two species of exotic game, the blackbuck antelope and the axis deer. When the ranch first started developing its exotic herds, it imported the finest. High quality game management and controlled hunting has resulted in some of the best trophy hunting in the state. Many think they're probably unmatched anywhere in the world.

It had been several months since I had been hunting. Two days is a normal allotment of time for an exotic big game hunt; however, I wanted to hunt so badly that I decided to work in a morning hunt at Onion Creek Lodge, with an afternoon trip to a Longhorn Cattle Auction at the YO in Mountain Home. The auction started at 2:00 o'clock, which meant I would need to be at Onion Creek bright and early, and heading out for Mountain Home by 11:00 o'clock.

I called Louis Schreiner, who books the exotic hunts at the YO, and scheduled Onion Creek for the morning of the auction. Since it was going to be such a short timespan, I decided to fly down. As you would expect, Onion Creek provides a pickup at the airport in Austin. But on Friday morning when I talked with the pilot, the weather report predicted storms and thunderheads. That's typical for Texas' spring. So I drove, leaving home in the middle of the night. I wanted to get in one more hunt before a hectic travel schedule closed out the next few months.

My son, Michael, and I, left the Clear Fork Ranch in Aledo at 3:00 a.m. With luck, we would be in Onion Creek between 7:00 and 8:00 o'clock.

One other thing I had done in preparation for the drive was to buy a radar detector. On the way home from my last hunting trip, I had let my foot get a little heavy. One of Texas' finest noticed and left me a stiff reminder. This time my "fuzz-buster" worked like a charm. In fact, we pulled up at the gate of the ranch around 7:15 a.m., which was not flying, but close to it.

As we pulled onto the paved road entry to the ranch, a sign said, "Lodge 3 miles," but don't believe it. My son, Michael, is convinced that it's at least five. But it's a scenic five mile drive and a great mental conditioner. Seeing deer and antelope along the way is not only a beautiful sight, it puts me in a hunting attitude. For certain, Onion Creek is, "Where the deer and the antelope play."

Within ten minutes we reached the main lodge of the ranch to find Lodge Manager, Bo Wafford, on the steps awaiting our arrival. He told us coffee and rolls were inside, but Michael and I had stopped on the way, and were ready to begin the hunt. Bo loaded us into the ranch wagon and we headed out.

Though there has never been an actual census of the exotic game population at Onion Creek, Bo said that Charley III (the head Schreiner) estimates around 1,500 blackbuck antelope and 1,000 axis deer. Though the animals keep their distance, it was evident as we began to drive safari-style through the ranch that abundant game was available.

The pasture looked lush despite the tough winter and the lack of rain. Only two days ago rain had begun to fall.

"We would have been in trouble in two or three weeks without it," according to Bo.

As we traveled across the ranch we began to see the axis and blackbuck antelope which Onion Creek is famous for. While we drove, Bo provided a description of the animals we were seeing. As we passed one good-sized axis buck, he said, "That one's only 24 inches." I smiled to myself and remembered that my very first axis had only an 18 inch set of antlers. At Onion Creek, anything less than a 25 inch spread on an axis buck is not fair game; and 30 inches is not unusual.

A light rain began to fall. As it did, the animals seemed to disappear. Bo explained, "They'll move into the woods and the brush, which means it's going to be hard to find them and especially hard to tell what size antlers they have." Since I had hunted axis before, Bo knew that I wanted record-class if at all possible. He assured me there were some quality bucks available.

He hesitated about getting out of the vehicle to hunt, thinking the rain would eventually stop. It not only continued, but increased in intensity.

It had been more than two months since I had picked up a gun. Worse, I wouldn't have another chance to hunt until late July. As the rain fell, I began feeling the pressure of the short time I had allotted. Finally, we decided to disregard it and go for a big axis, rain or not.

As we topped a hill, we spotted near the tree line a group of six or eight axis deer, with what looked to be at least four good bucks. Through the rain, we glassed them and determined that there was one genuinely acceptable buck among them.

Bo edged the truck closer. The rain kept falling. I looked at my watch. It was a little after 9:00 o'clock. By the time I made a kill, we dressed him, and went back to the lodge, it would be close to 11:00. Then we would clean up, drive the 100 miles to Mountain Home, as well as stop for lunch, and we'd barely make it by 2:00. That kind of pressure, plus the rain, caused me to plan something I had never done before: I stayed in the ranch wagon to shoot.

The deer were located in the edge of some tall undergrowth and young trees. Bo and I agreed on which one was the biggest. I drew down my sights and squeezed off a shot. The sound of the bullet indicated a sure hit. It had that certain "zap." One of the bucks had reared up as though he had been hit.

We jumped out and raced after them hoping to locate the one I thought I had hit. We crossed the creek, walked the banks and made almost a mile circle. But no blood, no deer, and no luck.

We came back to where we had started and examined the area. Our first concern was to determine if there was any blood or sign that the animal had been wounded. There was nothing. But lying on the ground close to the spot where I had shot, Bo found a fairly good sized tree limb that had one of its ends blown off. I realized then that the "zap" I had heard was the tree. Score one for the tree, zero for me, and the deer as free.

I muttered to myself as we went back to the truck, irritated that I had missed, and even more that I had tried to shoot from the truck. Everything I knew about exotic big game hunting underscored that shooting from a vehicle was not a sporting proposition and should not be practiced or encouraged. I knew if I had another chance, there was no way I was going to shoot from the truck. It served me right that I had missed.

We loaded back into the ranch wagon and began to look for another animal. The rain didn't make it easy. The animals had stopped their foraging and were taking cover under the trees as Bo had predicted. We trekked back and forth. Every time we located a buck, by the time we could get close enough to glass him he would be gone. Over and over, the same thing kept happening.

We kept going, and then came on two bucks, one of whom was lying down. This time we got out of the truck and inched up as close as possible. When we glassed them, we both agreed that the one on the ground was a good specimen. As we discussed the best way to approach him, Bo mentioned a concern of his. He said he'd never seen me totally miss a shot like I had earlier. Though we hadn't found any blood, he thought it might be possible that the buck on the ground was wounded and the one I had shot at before. We crawled up carefully, glassing him again. He looked good. I raised up on my knees to take aim. Just as I did, he heard us. He definitely was not wounded and took off just as I squeezed the trigger. Another miss!

I couldn't believe it. I had totally missed two in a row. It was upsetting. My son began to provide excuses for me about the rain, and the trees. I appreciated that, but the reality was I had missed.

We made our way back to the truck and began what seemed to be a fruitless circling back and forth across the ranch. Around 11 o'clock, we were hailed by R.B. Wilson, a frequent guide for the lodge. I had been so certain that I wanted only to book the morning that Bo had invited R.B. and his wife to make a trip with them that afternoon. None of us could believe we had been out that long without a kill. R.B. joined us in the truck and after assessing the situation offered some other suggestions for hunting spots.

Off we went and before long we jumped a large herd of does and bucks, with several possibilities among them. But they were not where we could get a shot. We left the vehicle and circled to get downwind. When we moved in, there was no sign of them. We checked our watches. I had decided if I could get to Mountain Home by 5:00 that would be soon enough. We talked over the best place to try again. R.B. suggested a creek not too far away, so we loaded in the truck and headed for it.

Sure enough, as we approached it, we could see in the distance a large herd heading across the creek the other way. They turned and looked at us and then started up the hill and faded into the trees.

R.B. volunteered to follow them through the trees while Bo and I circled back around.

We forded the creek, came up on the other side, and pulled down to where we anticipated R.B. and the deer would be heading. I got out of the truck and waited. Unfortunately, we had misjudged where we were. We finally spotted R.B. more than a quarter of a mile up the creek. The deer were long gone.

The time was getting close now. We had been out

more than five hours, and I would be lucky to get to Mountain Home at all if this kept up.

We loaded back into the truck and decided to try one more time. R.B. suggested a spot a mile or so away where he had noticed them foraging recently. We headed out, determined to give it one more good effort.

As we approached the area R.B. had mentioned, we spotted a large herd milling in the trees about a half mile away. I knew this was my last chance. We parked the wagon and got out, quietly circling as much downwind as possible. When we were about 400 yards away we glassed them. There were a lot of bucks in the group. Some of the biggest were still in velvet. We moved in closer and then I saw one that stood out above the rest. He was slightly hidden by the trees, but I felt confident he was a big one. Bo and R.B. agreed.

I glassed him one more time and then went to my .270. He was about 250 yards away and facing away from me. I aimed for his right front shoulder, hoping to break his shoulders. As I was aiming I could tell that I was hurrying my shot, but somehow I just couldn't slow down inside.

I squeezed the trigger; he was hit but not fatally. We ran after him and when he stopped inside the trees I took aim again. Zap! Off he went, valiantly fighting two heavy shots. Finally, 50 yards away, he slumped to the ground, but kept raising his head and trying to get up. I was genuinely frustrated that I had not been a better shot. I knelt down and carefully took aim. He didn't move again after that shot.

A. M. Micallef

Al, with son Michael (right) and Bo Wafford (left). This picture does not do justice to the magnificent axis deer. (In fact, the picture doesn't do me justice either.)

When we got to the clearing I was amazed at his size and his antlers. A quick measurement showed them to be 35 inches base to tip. And we guessed his weight on the hoof at 200 or more.

Bo quickly started dressing him and we loaded him onto the wagon. Once we were back at the lodge we weighed him in; dressed, he tallied 161 pounds which is a big axis deer.

Finally, I relaxed inside. I had the deer I wanted, and I had learned some important lessons about hunting exotic big game:

1. Rain makes animals very difficult to find and to hunt because they tend to bunch up in the trees and underbrush rather than foraging in the open.

2. Hunting, like any skill, requires practice. I should have gone to the practice range the day before.

3. Hurrying is bad for the hunter and the hunted. It creates the possibility of only wounding an animal and returning empty-handed for the hunt.

Fortunately, I had hunted Onion Creek before. I knew the quality of their accommodations, the food, and the guides. It's a rare experience. And though I had created unnecessary pressure on myself by trying to squeeze too much into one day, it had been a challenging hunt and ultimately a rewarding one. I was anxious to come back again to the YO's Onion Creek Lodge.

William Reaves, Lonestar Photography

Outstanding fallow, in velvet.

CHAPTER V

The Flying A Ranch:

quality, stability, and beauty.

Before traveling for the first time to the Flying A Ranch in Bandera, Texas, I visited by phone with the ranch manager, Emmit Schmidt. He told me of the hunting dates that were open and of the various species of exotic big game available. They included the fallow deer, red stag, blackbuck antelope, Corsican ram, axis deer, sika deer, and aoudad sheep. We agreed on a date, although I was still uncertain which animal I would hunt.

A few weeks later, on a Saturday morning in mid-February, I headed for Bandera. It's less than 50 miles from San Antonio, and should have been reachable by car in no more than five hours from my ranch in Aledo. But a pea-soup fog made travel slow and dangerous.

Finally, after seven hours, I reached Bandera, and in less than five minutes I was outside Bandera, nearing the edge of the Flying A Ranch.

As I approached, I saw cars stopped alongside the road viewing what looked like a hundred or more head of axis deer in a specially enclosed, non-hunting field. For someone who really likes wild animals, seeing this many exotic game in one place is a great feeling.

I pulled up to the giant iron gates of the headquarters, where I had been instructed to wait for Emmit. He arrived within minutes of our scheduled time. His pride in the 6,500 acres of beautiful, yet challenging hills, valleys, brush, and water that make up the ranch, was evident from our first meeting. I learned in visiting with him that he was formerly a public school educator and administrator, with a background in farming and land management as well. For the last twelve years he had managed the Flying A.

On this day, he had reserved the entire ranch for my hunt. I parked my vehicle, and climbed into the ranch hunting vehicle for a tour of the facilities, and hopefully a look at the animals available for hunting. It didn't take long to realize there was a lot of good quality game available, as well as the promise of a challenging hunt. Emmit suggested that we try to take a large spotted fallow deer that he had seen several times recently. The previous fall I had taken a brown and a white fallow deer; a spotted one would look good between them.

Too, the fallow deer is one of the world's most popular deer. It was transplanted in the 1930's from its native home near the Mediterranean region of Europe (close in fact to my parents' birthplace of Malta) to countries around the world. Now on any new game ranch fallow deer are one of the first exotics to be stocked. Its beautiful antlers — described as "palmated" due to their similarity to the palm of our hand — make great trophies. Although the fallow deer is one of the more easily domesticated of deer, Emmit promised a wild and wily buck.

It was still early in the morning when we set out on one of the many roads of the ranch. On each side of us, the brush and hills were full of various animals, viewing us with bored curiosity. I thought, **This is going to be too easy.** Then the ranch vehicle stopped and I stepped out.

Off the animals raced like the wild animals they were. I asked Emmit why they seemed so docile as the vehicle appeared, but totally wild when we stepped out. I learned that it was due in part to the supplemental feeding program the ranch had administered that winter. It had been the harshest winter on record, and without supplemental feeding a large segment of their game would have died. Fortunately, they had lost very few. The manner in which the feeding had been administered had not hindered the hunting.

I observed the feeding program and was most impressed. Feed spreaders were attached to the back of their trucks, and then pulled over the 32 miles of road covering the ranch without the staff ever leaving their vehicles. The speed with which this was accomplished not only made it efficient, but it also didn't create a familiarity on the part of the animals with any one feeding spot or with humans putting feed into troughs and bins.

We traveled for some time until Emmit spotted the buck he had mentioned. I glassed him and immediately knew I wanted him, which he must have sensed, for we had hardly put our glasses on him until he and another buck and some does disappeared from sight.

Fortunately, Emmit knew the ranch backwards and forwards. So we started slowly crisscrossing the vast acreage safari style. Soon we had spotted the group of animals our quarry was traveling with. They were on top of a good sized hill to our left. We glassed them for a few seconds before they disappeared again. Emmit felt certain they would still be on the hill. We parked, careful not to slam the doors and then began slowly trekking up the hillside.

Walking behind Emmit, I soon picked up his almost tiptoe style of walking as we attempted both to keep from alerting the deer as well as wanting to stay downwind of them.

After a half hour or so, we reached the top of the hill, but we could see nothing. Suddenly, through the brush and trees, an axis buck and two doe came racing, almost running into us. They were as startled by seeing us as we were them. They made an abrupt change of direction and dashed through the woods. Their panic meant there was no chance of our buck's sticking around, if indeed he had been there from the first.

We forged on to a clearing and tried to glass the area for the direction the buck might have gone, but with no luck. So back to the vehicle and trying again. As we kept driving, we encountered some beautiful red deer, some great-looking blackbuck antelope, as well as an abundance of axis. But our group of fallow deer had evidently sensed the hunting pressure and were no where in sight despite Emmit's familiarity with the land and the animals. We pushed to the outskirts of the preserve and determined to make one more try before lunch.

No luck.

The time had become a complicating factor for me now since I had allotted only one day for this hunt. I had to leave Bandera that night due to an overseas business trip the following day that couldn't be delayed.

I don't know if **Murphy's Law** is operative in hunting or not, but there always seems to be a direct correlation between the amount of time I have available to hunt and the difficulty of the hunt I'm on. The more time I have, the less difficult the hunt is; the less time, the more difficult.

The year before, I had fourteen days reserved to hunt brown bear in Alaska. Would you believe I bagged a nine-footer my first day out! Just the reverse has happened other times: I've gone out for a short hunt of a day or two and seen everything but the one animal I wanted. At the moment, it looked like my fallow deer would fall in the latter category. While at lunch, I called my office to alert them that I might be arriving at the Bandera airport later than scheduled. With some cooperation from the sun, I was determined to bag this fallow.

About an hour and a half into the afternoon Emmit thought he caught a glimpse of our buck with about five or six others. We stopped and again began the slow process of stalking, hoping not to arouse them to our presence.

As we inched forward, we periodically glassed the group, but they were in heavy underbrush and trees which made it difficult not only to identify them, but also to know for sure that the buck we were hunting was in the group. After all, there were several hundred head of animals on the ranch. That our's would be in this group would have to be determined by getting closer than we had thus far without disturbing them.

Finally, we confirmed that this looked like the same bunch we had seen that morning, but we still couldn't locate the buck we were looking for. After a long search we thought we found him bedded down in the middle of the other deer. But, the trees, the other animals around him, and his being on the ground didn't give me a shot. That meant we had not only to get him off the ground, but also exposed in such a way that I could get off a good shot.

As we moved in closer, one of the animals sensed our presence and moved nervously. My buck jumped to his feet and began to pace around. Emmit and I glassed him carefully. I was relatively certain he was what we were after and Emmit agreed. The problem would be making a kill shot. The trees and brush were so thick I could hardly distinguish between them and the deer.

They were spooked, though, and I knew that it was probably now or never on this hunt. I nodded to Emmit that I wanted to try to take him.

Difficult shot — just reasonable fallow.

A. M. Micallef

Since I had never hunted with Emmit before I'm sure he had some reservations about my percentages on such a shot. As I put my scope on them, he asked if I felt I could get him. I nodded my head.

Just then the deer began to trot out of their covering and I saw a brief opening between some trees and the underbrush. I drew down on the big buck, then led him ever so slightly, hoping to hit him just behind the front left leg and into the heart.

I squeezed the trigger and he leaped forward. For a few seconds I was not sure I had a kill. He travelled for 50 yards or so and then fell. We were still more than 150 yards away and I could see his head. I was fairly certain my first shot had been on target, but just in case it wasn't, I knelt down and aimed a shot at his neck. That did it. (If I hadn't been successful, I saw Emmit coming up behind me with a rifle. One thing consistent about all the guides on Texas game ranches: they don't want a wounded animal lost in the bushes.)

Emmit went back to the vehicle, while I hurried over to the animal. He had a fine set of flattened palmated antlers that measured 32 inches. And although not record book quality ("ground shrinkage" was Emmit's way of explaining how big he had looked in the glasses compared to after the kill!), he would make a fine addition to my two other fallow deer.

Soon Emmit was back with the ranch vehicle and pulled out his knife to begin dressing my kill. I wanted both a mounting and the meat. Emmit had kept no records of how many hundred animals he had dressed in his 12 years at the Flying A, but it was easy to see it had been plenty. Within a matter of five minutes or less, the deer was split open, disembowled and ready for loading.

The dressing revealed that my first shot had indeed been a kill shot penetrating the lower quarter of the heart. The second shot was insurance only.

We drove back to where we had started the hunt. Soon Emmit was joined by one of his staff and they hoisted the buck up and washed him out, then moved him into the cooler. Later, they would drop him by one of the many packing plants available. From there the head mount would be delivered to my favorite taxidermist from where he would be sent off for tanning. In six months or so I would have a spotted fallow deer ready for my trophy wall.

Emmit and I shook hands, and within minutes I was heading for the Bandera airport. Once airborne, I asked the pilot to fly over the Flying A. It was even more beautiful from the air.

A permanent image of the Flying A had been formed: **class and quality.** The game management, the ranch itself, and the superior animals available were all an exceptional example of an exotic big game hunting program.

That must have been the aim of owner Albert B. Alkek when he acquired the ranch in 1961. He built superior containment structures, as well as introducing the best of game management principles. The result has been an unbroken commitment to conservation and the preservation and development of wildlife.

The Flying A was a great place to hunt. But this hunt was over. In a few weeks, I would be joining one of East Africa's professional white hunters, Finn Aagaard, for a "fair chase" hunt at the Buttery ranch, near Llano. But for now I was ready to sit back, relax and enjoy the trip home. Or so I thought.

It turned out to be the most harrowing flight I've ever had in a small plane. An unpredicted storm hit the area around the airport we were going to use. High winds and hail sounded like they would tear the plane up. The ceiling was so low that we had to search for the landing strip. When we found it, I tripped the runway lights on with a portable device for use when the airport is closed. Just as we were approaching for landing, the timer on the lights ran out and the runway was enveloped in darkness and hail. We swung back again, determined to hold off on the light switch until we were certain we were close to the ground.

It was a hairy feeling. We kept descending for what seemed like forever. When I did flip the switch, the field lighted up and we were less than 75 yards away. Touch down and wait for the hail to be over. Flying to London the next day would seem like a piece of cake!

A. M. Micallef

Very nice record book mouflon, and great hunt with Finn Aagaard.

CHAPTER VI

Finn Aagaard:

hunting in Llano, Texas with an African White Hunter.

One of the exciting things about hunting is the variety it offers. No hunt is the same. The animals, the weather, the place, the chase: all have their uniqueness.

But one of the genuinely unique experiences is to hunt with a world class professional hunter and safari outfitter from Kenya, East Africa — and to do it right in the Lone Star State.

I'm meaning, Finn Aagaard, a native Kenyan, who left East Africa when excessive poaching caused all big game hunting to be closed down. Finn and his lovely wife Berit, and their three children, left Kenya in 1978 and came to the New Africa, Hill Country, Texas.

The first time Finn guided a hunt at one of the Hill Country ranches, he said, "I knew that this was the right place for me. It was so like Kenya that it was unbelievable — big and rough — the game wild and free. Just the place to maintain exotic game hunting that would compare closely with African hunting."

Together with Dunlop Farren, a good friend, old client, Houston businessman and a long-time hunter, they set up Wildlife Safaris, Inc., and negotiated with Dr. H. D. Buttery and Mr. Jim Inks to offer exotic game safaris on their adjoining Bar-O and Inks ranches in Llano, Texas, the deer capitol of the world.

Hunting on the two ranches meant a combined 12,000 acres of rugged and scenic granite hills, cut up by sand rivers and brush draws, with mesquite and oak covered slopes and flats. Though there are a few fences, they are not game-proof, and the animals can range freely over the whole.

Before long the word had spread, and every game ranch and trophy hunter learned about the special dimensions of hunting with Finn Aagaard. His specialty: "fair chase."

And if anyone ever misunderstood Texas big game hunting to be some kind of driving around in a chauffered car to find an animal of choice which could be shot from the car window, they have only to meet Finn to refute that gross misconception.

According to Finn, there have always been those kinds of hunts available, even in Africa. There were plenty of guides who were more than willing to set up blinds at watering holes where the hunter would wait for the animals to appear and then make his kill. To Finn, that was not really hunting, and for certain, not fair chase hunting. Balancing the hunt, and emphasizing the chase, is what hunting is all about to Finn.

Consequently, when everyone said you can't write a book about exotic big game hunting in Texas without having hunted with Finn Aagaard, I took their advice and made my reservation. From my first telephone conversation, I knew we had a straight talking, no frills, hunting pro with little or no time for the less than serious hunter.

Finn met me in his very used GMC pickup (no showy Zebra painted Land Rover, for sure). We drove for 20 to 30 minutes until we were well into Hill Country. Finn told me that at one time the ranch we were heading for had been a giant 120,000 acre spread. Now some of it is a state park, and other parts of it have been divided into smaller ("Texas small") ranches of a few thousand acres.

The Aagaard residence had formerly been the headquarters for the original ranch and had been built around the turn of the century. Though it had not been lived in for more than seven years before the Aagaards arrived, their special touch had given it a unique aura. And by the time I had consumed one of Finn's breakfasts, (eggs from their own hens, ham from a wild hog shot by his son, and Berit's unbelievable homemade bread) I was ready to go.

From the first, there was something about Finn that I knew would make this hunt different from any I'd been on before. I think part of it comes from his being a world-class hunter, with more than 30 years of professional hunting experience. It provides him an ease and confidence in guiding hunters that is unique. For example, sighting in my gun. The year before I hunted more than 30 times; I regularly practice on my range at home; and I felt quite confident about the sighting of my .270. Most times, on other hunts, I've been asked if I needed to sight my gun. Without exception, I've always replied no.

Finn didn't ask. He took me down to the river and a very simple target range: a table, box, and 150 yards away, a DUZ soap box filled with sand, with a target taped to it. That was my first surprise. I'd spent a fortune on hunting equipment, and if I had been building the range, it would never have entered my mind to use a soap box.

Finn then handed me some airline type ear guards. When I said I wouldn't need them, he replied, "I learned that I needed them a little too late," referring to the hearing loss he has. (I now use them every time I'm practicing.)

We calibrated the adjustment I needed at 150 yards and I squeezed off a few rounds. Finn seemed satisfied and soon we were in his GMC heading into some of the most rugged territory I have seen in Texas.

First, was a river that had to be forded. Finn's GMC did not have four-wheel drive so that meant: ready, set, and go like hell! Next, we began to navigate what he assured me were roads. The rocks were so immense that the pickup leaned, groaned, and slowly climbed.

Periodically, the incline was too steep which meant backing up and starting over, only faster. There were giant boulders matching anything in Colorado's Garden of the Gods, breathtaking views of rocks, hills, plateaus, trees, growth of all kinds, underbrush, you name it.

There were also some very wild mouflon ram with marvelous coats and beautiful horns. When I asked Finn what kind of hunting they would provide, he smiled and said, "The very best." He went on to explain that these wild mountain sheep had never had even supplemental feeding. They are free-living, naturally-reproducing populations that have been well established for at least 30 years. In all respects they are true wild game that offer as sporting a hunt here as they ever did in their original homelands in the mountains of Sardinia and Corsica.

Finn initially felt he knew where we could find a herd with some good-sized rams in it. He had seen them the week previous. According to him, mouflon tended to stake out an area and stay near it. So off we went.

Every now and then he would see a movement, which meant stop, get out and glass it. We would then determine that it was not what he was looking for. After awhile we reached the top of a very high hill and glassed the area for some time. No sign of any mouflon, but we did see some magnificent country, several aoudad, some sika deer and fallow deer, as well as whitetail deer.

Back in the truck again.

And so it went for the rest of the day. We broke for lunch and then went back on the prowl again. This time we took a four-wheel drive vehicle. Periodically, we would sight some animals in the distance, leave the truck and then gradually work ourselves downwind. Each time though, the animals had sensed the pressure. By the time we had worked around close enough to be in range they would be gone.

We were close to losing daylight when we spotted a small herd of rams about half a mile away. We sighted them and counted five rams, with one or two that looked like excellent specimens. We left the truck and began our downwind trek. Initially, I wasn't as careful about the noise level as I should have been; I didn't realize how close Finn was getting us. We circled around in such a way that caused me to lose my direction. We worked through some dry creek beds and underbrush, climbed some small hills and crossed some valleys. Then Finn motioned to me and pointed to our quarry no more than than 50 to 75 yards away.

The best one of the group was partially hidden behind a big cedar bush. The only portion of its body that I could see was its hind quarter which wouldn't offer a kill shot. Then Finn motioned me up and pointed to a different angle and place from which to shoot. Unfortunately, it was already inhabited by a prickly pear bush, which distracted me momentarily.

Finally, though, I managed to position myself where the ram's front quarter was exposed. I could see his horns and about three inches past his front leg. He was beginning to move away from us. I aimed about two inches behind his shoulder and low enough to catch the top half of the heart and the lungs.

As I squeezed the shot off, the ram spun and ran down the hill out of our sight. I felt certain that I had seen a spurt of blood when the bullet penetrated and was positive that he would be no more than 25 yards away.

When we reached where he had been, there was an easily observable trail of blood. We found him less than 20 yards away. He had a beautiful coat, an excellent set of horns, and was about as purebred a mouflon as I had seen in Texas. Finn quickly dressed him and confirmed that I did have a heart and lung shot. I beamed like a school boy when Finn said, "A perfect shot."

I had bagged bigger animals, and more trophy class animals, but never had more fun doing it. And as we drove back to the house, I realized the difference had been Finn. Adding to the fun had been his family, two sons and daughter, and his incredible wife, Berit.

It was she who met us when we drove in. To my surprise, within minutes she had her knife out and had caped the ram quicker and more expertly than any one I had ever seen from here to Alaska. Though she was the daughter of an ambassador who had also been the chief of protocol for the Norwegian government, there was no squeamishness, only quick, deft, and effective strokes.

When they asked me about the meat, I said that I had never tried mouflon. They smiled, and a little while later we sat down to a candlelight dinner of some mouflon steak from their stock that was tastier than any game meat I had ever eaten.

It was a storybook day — and one I hope to repeat many times, both there and on the other ranches which Finn works with. But the hunt is what it's all about. And I've never had better.

The next day I planned to fly for home. For some reason, I was having great weather for hunting, but lousy luck to and from. Two hunts previous, I had run into the worst hail storm I'd ever flown in. The next hunt, I had pea-soup fog on the way down and on the way back I was stopped for speeding. And then on this trip, we were delayed two hours on takeoff because of weather. When we did reach Weatherford, the runway was fogged in, which meant some hairy rerouting to Ft. Worth.

But hunting with Finn Aagaard was worth it — fog, thorns, and all!

CHAPTER VII

Bryan Coleman:

hunting for aoudad in Texas with a Professional White Hunter

Few of us will ever have the opportunity to hunt big game in Africa; and with the closing of legalized hunting in such areas as Kenya and Uganda, little remains of the hunting challenges that once thrived on the dark continent. In the countries that are still open, such as Zambia, where I recently hunted, and Tanzania, informed opinions are that the hunting only slightly resembles Africa's hunting heydays. Most predict that it is only a matter of time before the whole of Africa will be closed forever to big game hunting.

That's why it's all the more exciting to have a hunting experience rooted in the African tradition of the past. That was my experience when hunting with Bryan Coleman, a Professional White Hunter from Kenya.

Our aoudad hunt took place at the Valdena Farms, near Utopia, Texas, which unfortunately has since changed ownership. Hundreds of years ago, this area of south Texas and the rugged Hill Country were favorite hunting grounds of the nomadic Commanches and the Lipa Apaches. They were attracted by the mild climate, the rich ground cover, and the variety of terrain, both level and rolling. The region's similarity to many of Africa's finest hunting areas offered a natural habitat for several varieties of exotic big game.

I arrived at the ranch in late afternoon and met Bryan and his family. Bryan's hunting exploits in his native homeland, as well as the Sudan, Zaire, Zambia and Indonesia are the stuff from which books are made. On this particular day he brought to bear his 25 years of hunting experience to produce a genuinely unique hunting experience for me.

The style of hunting was my choice. With a guide like Bryan available, I couldn't pass up a fair-chase hunt on foot.

My goal was to bag one of their trophy aoudad, the most elusive of wild mountain sheep in the world. Bryan assured me that the hunting experience would be as good as any aoudad hunting anywhere, bar none.

The area in which we chose to hunt was very hilly and the terrain was varied. Before we started the hunt, Bryan made sure that I understood that with him there was no such thing as a guaranteed **kill.** He would guarantee a **hunt** of the highest quality, but beyond that it was to be the same as hunting in Africa: the results would depend upon the game found and the resources and skill of the hunter.

With Bryan as with Finn Aagaard, Texas's other noted PH from Kenya, they are as concerned with the quality of the hunt as they are the animal hunted. That may mean something other than a record book animal, but whatever the kill the hunter is assured of a rewarding hunt. Given a choice, my preference is a great hunt. Bryan understood that was the kind of hunting challenge I wanted, so off we went.

We drove several miles in his open ranch wagon before halting at the base of a heavily covered hill. We jumped out of the wagon and began the hunt. After we had gained some height, we were able to look down into a lush valley and discover two big rams grazing approximately a mile away. Unfortunately, they spotted us as well and immediately disappeared into the bush. The challenge of tracking an animal through the tough Texas hillside was on.

Observing Bryan tracking was a thing of beauty. He kept his eye out for animal droppings, as well as observing the bent grass and broken limbs. And a first for me, he kept **smelling** the air for a scent. He would cup his hand and try to move the air through his nostrils.

After a half hour or so of working our way through fairly thick underbrush and trees, Bryan felt he had located a herd of bachelor rams which the two rams we had seen earlier were probably part of. They were in a ravine 100 or so yards away.

We slowed down and positioned ourselves to be downwind and then began a careful trek forward toward a ledge from which we could get a shot. I cupped my hands as I had seen Bryan do, and sure enough, I could detect a faint smell of a goat or sheep. Like domestic goats, old ram aoudads throw off a strong odor. Tracking them by smell was an interesting new dimension in hunting for me.

When we were less than 50 yards from the ledge which we were moving towards, a sika deer broke for cover and began "barking" as though he'd been shot. There was a thunderous sound of hoofbeats as our aoudads fled the ravine below.

There was not much choice but to keep pursuing them, though we knew it would be much more difficult now that they were feeling the pressure of the hunt. We kept working until we had picked up their track again. Bryan periodically checked their spore and kept us on path. Invariably, when we would get close, the same sika deer — the watchdog of the "forest" — would bark again.

This pattern kept repeating itself until lunch time. Finally, we decided to quit and start over later. Bryan informed us that it would be a waste of our time to hunt during the hottest part of the day. The animals would be bedded down, which would make them almost impossible to find. So we went back to the lodge to wait until later in the afternoon.

Around 4:00 o'clock, Bryan picked us up again. He suggested we start this time by checking several of their watering holes, which we proceeded to do. After a walk of a half mile or so we were able to position ourselves to glass one of the watering areas. No animals of any kind were in sight. On the way to the second one, Bryan spotted what he thought were fresh droppings on the trail. We proceeded to move very quietly and slowly until we were within 250 or 300 yards of the watering site. Then, on our hands and knees, we spent the next 15 or 20 minutes crawling less than 25 yards. We kept trying to keep the brush and trees between us and them. Fortunately, the wind was to our face.

The direction from which we had come provided almost no vegetation between us and the watering hole which meant we couldn't get much closer than 250 yards. They were bunched up together and I was convinced that I could get off a good shot, but while I was watching one of them caught sight of us and in milliseconds the whole herd had disappeared.

For the novice, that would have been the end of the line for this herd, but not Bryan. Once again we started tracking. After another hour and a half Bryan smiled and whispered that they had evidently made a complete circle and were heading back to the same watering area. While we were carefully inching toward the watering area, another herd ran past us toward the ravine that we had been in earlier that morning. I thought we would take after it, but Bryan said he was certain there was still another herd heading for the watering area. We kept inching forward. This time we were still downwind but our approach gave us better cover.

When we were less than 150 yards away we were able to glass the area. There was a herd of 25 or more watering quietly. We inched closer. At about 100 yards, Bryan pointed out a very respectable aoudad near the edge of the herd with horns of probably 30 inches or more. I shook my head no because there was an old ram in the center of the herd that I was confident had horns that would measure 33 or 34 inches. There were some tree limbs in the way, but I knew I could clear those by shooting a little lower than normal and still have a good heart shot.

I sighted him in and squeezed off a round. One of the herd jumped straight up in the air and took off running. I was amazed when he didn't drop on the spot. As the herd raced to the underbrush and trees, I kept expecting him to fall. As close as I had been, and with that good an aim, I knew that he was a seriously wounded animal.

We searched for more than an hour. No blood, no tracks, nothing to indicate a mortal wound. Finally, we went back to the area where I had taken my shot.

Nothing. Then Bryan found my "kill" — a bullet hole through the limb of a tree! I had hit the danged tree! Obviously, the size of the tree limb and the hole through it, meant the bullet had mushroomed on impact, and had been virtually harmless when it had come out the other side of the limb. Earlier, Bryan had said that he had heard a "crack" sound instead of the normal "thump" of a bullet hitting an animal. The "crack" had obviously been my bullet hitting the tree limb. The leaping aoudad had been hit by the spent bullet which had only enough velocity to sting, but nothing more. It was Bryan's opinion that it probably would not even have broken the heavy skin of the aoudad, which is why we found no blood of any kind.

Needless to say, I was greatly disappointed that I didn't have an aoudad to show for the day's hunting. But, it had been one heck of a hunt. Bryan Coleman was a super guide. I had nothing really to complain about other than having made a bad shot.

We hunted a little while longer, but the approaching dusk meant it would be unwise to keep up the hunt, so we called it quits. After expressing my gratitude to Bryan for such a quality hunting experience, we shook hands, and soon I was heading north. It had been another super hunting day in Texas, with one of the finest guides I've ever been with, Bryan Coleman.

William Reaves, Lonestar Photography

Another grand axis. As you can tell, I am partial to axis deer.

CHAPTER VIII

Greenwood Valley Ranch:

a rugged ranch and super people.

When first beginning this book, there was one ranch that everyone said I would have to hunt: **Greenwood Valley.** But as I listened to them describe the ranch, I realized something very interesting about what they were saying. They talked more about the **managers** of the ranch than they did the ranch. They did say that the ranch was some of the most challenging land anywhere: literally a rocky expanse of 16,000 acres. And the game, they said, especially the axis deer, rivalled that of the countries from which they had been imported. Furthermore the accommodations were outstanding.

But the one thing that kept being repeated over and over was how terrific the ranch managers, Jeff and Fernne Hunt were. That was my experience exactly. I went to the ranch to hunt and went away fans of the Hunts.

That does not mean the ranch is not a super place to hunt. Greenwood Valley is incredibly challenging. It is rugged in the extreme. The average elevation is 2,200 feet. There's never enough rain and what does come is not predictable. There are high hills and low valleys, all nestled close to the head waters of the Nueces River. Four-wheel drive vehicles are a must. There are thousands of oak trees, sheer limestone cliffs, rocky canyons, juniper shrub, pinon pine, and the green of the mountain laurel.

Furthermore, it's a stable program. It was first stocked with exotic game in the early 1950's. Exotic game ranges free on more than 16,000 acres of Real County, Texas, some of the toughest in Texas. And most importantly, the owners of the ranch, V.E. Cook and John Wootters, have provided the Hunts with both the resources and the commitment to insure that Greenwood Valley maintains the best of wildlife management principles. As a result, the ranch consistently has developed a quality of game which improves year after year.

That's a thumbnail sketch of the ranch; no such words would do for the Hunt's. They simply have to be the nicest people I've met anywhere, bar none. Their special quality was first revealed when I drove for five miles from the highway to the locked gate of the ranch. A pickup truck was standing in the gate. Waiting patiently for our arrival was Jeff Hunt!

At the ranch, Fernne was there to meet us and offer us coffee and cake. Since she serves as the secretary to the Exotic Wildlife Association, her inquiries as to how our hunting was going were informed and helpful. That orientation to be of help never let up. In fact, from the minute we set foot on the ranch until we left the following day, there was nothing that could have been done for us that wasn't done. The Hunt's are quality, quality people.

Even though the Hunts themselves overshadow the ranch, Greenwood Valley is a super place to hunt. Unlike many, it is a "working" exotic big game ranch. Every year, several hundred game are trapped and sold either to replenish or start the stock of other game ranches. All trophy animals are kept.

This pattern of keeping the best has been developed over a period of more than thirty years and has resulted in the upgrading of Greenwood Valley's game to that of one of the premier stocks in Texas. It includes axis deer from India, fallow deer from Europe, European red stag, blackbuck antelope from India, aoudad sheep from North Africa, nilgai antelope from India, Corsican sheep from the Mediterranean, and Iranian/Nubian ibex.

Finn Aagaard, formerly of Kenya, and now a guide and partner in Wildlife Safaris, has described Greenwood Valley in the most positive superlatives. He said, "The number of animals seen and the variety of species reminds me of some of the better hunting areas of my native country, Kenya." Other professionals such as John Wootters of *Petersen's Magazine* have echoed the same sentiments.

What all of this means for the exotic big game hunter is the availability of everything it takes to make a good hunt: great game, super land, and excellent accommodations. Of all the places I've hunted, I'm convinced there is not a better place to engage in fair-chase than at Greenwood Valley. Both times I've been at Greenwood Valley, the weather and the time restraints did not permit a fair-chase hunt. Nonetheless, it was a very satisfying hunt.

The hunt I did take was safari style with a goal of taking a trophy axis. I spent one afternoon and the balance of the next morning searching for a truly great one. What I saw were axis that every other ranch would say were great. But Jeff and Fernne's son-in-law, Jerry Andis, who was my guide for this trip, kept saying "There are some better ones, Just wait."

I thought we were going to wait too long. But each time we topped a hill or cliff and saw a good axis, Jerry would say, "There's a better one."

Finally, when we were several miles into the cliffs and hills of the ranch, Jerry said, "Let's try a spot that I don't think anyone's been into for a year or more." I agreed while hoping to myself that we would find something soon.

We were at one of the highest elevations on the ranch when Jerry spotted a buck about a quarter of a mile away. We left the ranch wagon and began moving forward. Fortunately, we were in a crosswind from the buck and moving up the hill.

When we were less than 125 yards away, I was afraid to wait any longer. The buck's head was framed in an opening in the trees. Below a tree branch I could see a part of his chest cavity. I squeezed the trigger. The

A. M. Micallef

After an exciting stalk, took this outstanding axis. A pleasurable experience.

sound of the cartridge exploding echoed through the rockfilled cliffs. The buck sprang forward and was instantly lost in the trees.

We hurried forward, anxious not to lose him. We examined where he had been standing and found blood. With the help of Jerry, I began following the path he had left. Less than 100 yards away, we saw him stretched out on the ground.

Jerry insisted we wait a few minutes and not crowd him. Then he carefully walked up and checked him out. He was dead. When we measured him, I was well satisfied not only with his antlers, but the condition he was in. That would mean a lot when he went to the processors.

That's also one of the great things about this deer: axis meat is some of the finest game meat on the hoof. In fact, they're the best of any, in my opinion. It's usually very lean and when dressed out, it makes excellent table meat. For certain, it's a lot healthier than the typical steaks and hamburger bought at the store.

Too, I get very tired of the Texas palate: Mexican food and chicken fried steak soon lose their appeal. A lean piece of meat from a good axis deer has the flavor of an animal that's lived on acorns, browsed on grass and lived on natural things. It's a real taste experience to me. Now that I've gotten used to the lean taste of game, I have a bodily reaction to the grain fed, high fat beef in most stores and restaurants. This axis was headed for the Micallef freezer for certain.

Jerry and I dressed him, then loaded him on the wagon. He was going to finish out at 250 pounds, at least. We headed back to the lodge where they cleaned him up and put him in the freezer. The next day they would take him in to Woodbury's for the antlers to be mounted and the meat to be taken to the processors.

Jeff and Fernne were there to meet us and congratulate us on the hunt. Naturally, Fernne had a snack for us before we hit the road. Soon, we were ready to say our goodbyes. This was only my second trip. It felt like leaving home. But I knew with the hospitality and the hunting at Greenwood Valley, I would be back before long.

A very nice Russian boar, and an exciting hunt.

A. M. Micallef

CHAPTER IX

Indian Creek:

a record book Russian boar.

Kerrville, Texas may well be the center of the state for hunting. There are outfitters of all kinds, rows and rows of taxidermists, and an environment which encourages both hunting and hunters.

One of the reasons it's such a hunter's paradise is the large number of hunting ranches which can be reached by vehicle in minutes. These ranches all have a uniqueness to them. Sometimes it's the land; other times, the game; or it may simply be the staff and the facilities. But after hunting many of them, I've learned they're as different as can be and usually have one area they're strong in.

The Indian Creek Ranch, just outside Kerrville, is generally recognized for the uniqueness of its wild boar hunts. It has the dogs, the game, and the land to make boar hunting a genuinely significant hunting experience.

I had never before hunted European-Russian boar. My inquiries had led me to believe that Indian Creek was the best place to try. I scheduled a hunt with Gregory Meyer, the young ranch manager, and arrived with my son Michael in time to get a tour of the ranch's facilities before the next day's early morning boar hunt.

The lodge we spent the night in was outstanding. It had a well-equipped kitchen, a spacious den, a large dining room with a full bay window, plus enough beds to sleep a large hunting party.

Greg had begun an ambitious hunting program in the three years he and his father had owned the ranch. They had just completed building a locker and meat dressing facility that was among the best I'd seen anywhere.

Though the potential is there, the ranch does not as yet have a long-term game management program. In fact, when animals are not available to the hunter's specifications, Greg trucks them in from the outside.

However, quality boar hunts appear to have been in operation at the ranch for a long period of time. The dogs and guides available seemed well qualified.

We were told to be ready by 6:30 the next morning. We grabbed a bite to eat and met our guide, Richard Grona, and his assistant, Gary. The dogs were ready. These were veteran dogs that had been on many hunts. Several had scars from their encounters with the vicious tusks of the boar. Richard told me they had at times run themselves to exhaustion rather than quit hunting. They were ready and eager to go this time.

We had two trucks, which had radio communications, and in addition, portable two-ways. Due to the concern of the dog handlers for their dogs, Richard insisted upon open-sighted guns.

We reached a range that was almost an entire section, which meant it ran a mile in each direction. It had an eight foot high wire fence encircling, and was locked and secure. The ground was a solid mass of trees, thorn bushes, and a ground cover that was almost impenetrable.

Richard took the dogs and drove to another part of the pasture. He said he would release them there and then we would wait until we heard their baying, to let us know when they had jumped a boar. We would then coordinate by radio and locate them by their barking. He emphasized again that because of the terrain and the importance of the dogs' safety, I was not to shoot until he or one of his assistants gave the word.

We waited for 15 to 20 minutes. We were positioned on some high ground overlooking the hunting range. It was a cool, overcast morning. We heard some barking and then word came over the radio from Richard that he had released the dogs. Before long we could pick up the sounds of their barking and yapping as they hunted for a scent. Gary explained that Richard would not let all the dogs loose until the others needed some help.

Suddenly, there was a dramatic shift in the sound of the dogs. Instead of the routine barking, there was now an intense and loud baying.

"They've got him now," said Gary. He checked in by radio with Richard who told him to sit tight until we knew which way they were headed.

Just as quickly as the baying had begun, it stopped. Richard called on the radio to ask if we were hearing anything. We answered negatively.

He said he was releasing the other dogs. Again, we heard the barking and yapping sounds. Then quiet. Finally, Richard radioed us to come down where he was. We went back to the truck and after driving a half mile or more found where Richard had parked.

"I don't know what's happened to them, but sooner or later, one of them is going to pick up a scent. So you and Bob go on into the thicket and be in place in case they come close."

I agreed. Gary was told to stay in place and to use the two-way if anything happened. About that time one of the original dogs came up. He acted exhausted.

"I'll be damned," said Richard. "That's the first time that's ever happened. We've got a smart pig on our hands if he outsmarted Winston."

Winston didn't seem to care. He seemed totally tired.

Richard and I started off. We went a quarter mile or so and then we heard them. It sounded like every dog in the country was in the thickets on the trail of this wild pig.

"Let's go!" said Richard.

That was easier said than done. The thickets had such a heavy undergrowth that at times it required crawling on hands and knees, other times going in circles. But we were getting closer to the dogs and the boar.

Suddenly, "Watch out! That's him!"

Almost without warning, there were dogs barking and baying and running around in a circle in front of me. I could hear the grunting of the boar but I couldn't see him.

Richard yelled, "Get him before he runs — and don't hit the dogs."

I pulled my rifle to my eye, and tried to find the pig. Then I saw him. He was a mean-looking Russian boar with a vicious set of tusks. I made sure there were no dogs in front and then I squeezed off a shot, right into the chest and heart.

The dogs rushed in immediately, as did Gary, who had just now reached us. They leashed the dogs and we grabbed the boar by his hind legs and started dragging him out.

If I had thought it was tough coming in, it was nothing compared to going back out. He was a big pig. Plus, something totally unexpected: he was covered with fleas! In seconds, my hands and arms had fleas all over them. I was more than glad to let Richard and Gary take my place.

It took a while, but we finally pulled him into a clearing. We tried wiping the fleas off, and then began to examine the boar. He was impressive. We measured his tusks and they were almost six inches in length.

Richard checked all his dogs and none had cuts. "That's a rarity," he said with a smile. They watered and fed the dogs, then loaded the boar. They guessed him to be around 150 pounds.

We headed back to the lodge where Greg met us. He was most enthusiastic when he saw the boar. "That's the biggest one I've ever seen taken here."

They promised to take it to the taxidermist for me. I double-checked arrangements on a beautiful chocolate fallow deer I had taken at the ranch the day before. The arrangements for both seemed satisfactory. I settled with Greg and soon was on my way. That had been my first boar hunt, but I hoped not the last.

The next day I was at Woodbury's, the taxidermy of the YO. They were very complimentary of both kills — the fallow's color and rack, and the size and weight of my boar. Their response was icing on the cake to a fun hunt.

William Reaves, Lonestar Photography

Blackbuck antelope is, in my opinion, the most regal of all the antelope. Truly my favorite exotic.

CHAPTER X

The Triple 777:

a five curl blackbuck antelope.

Due to the significant advertising program of the Triple 777 Ranch in Hondo, I knew they had an extensive game program with a reputation for being a well managed game ranch. They also had a reputation for participating in the different game conservation programs in the state. And too, I knew that their owner, Slim (he's almost 7 feet tall) Crapps, was an avid big game hunter himself. Equally important, he participates in the management of the ranch itself, which is somewhat unusual in many of the game ranching operations.

My son, Michael, and Catherine Mann, a longtime friend and writer, accompanied us on the trip to Hondo. Cathy's bestseller, *Tinsel Town,* had just been released, and she was beginning research on a new book which featured a Texan who loved to hunt. When I learned about it, I invited her to join us on the hunt at the Triple 777.

Once there, it was obvious that their game quality was excellent. They have a large population of blackbuck antelope, fallow, axis, mouflon, and Corsican rams. For example, their axis population would number close to 600, with probably 400 aoudad. Their sika deer are among the best I've seen in Texas. And one of the things that spoke really well was their program of breeding Dybowski sika, the largest of the 13 species of sika deer. This species of sika is relatively rare in Texas. Though they are not available for hunting yet, as the ranch's herd grows and they have adequate replacement breeding stock, these will become an outstanding hunting experience.

The animals available for hunting have been on the ranch for many years and have adapted very well. They react in much the same way they would in their native habitat. The ranch breeds and raises these animals for harvest in the way that you feel it should be done. (Though the four-horned sheep is not an exotic, The Triple 777 has the largest herd I've seen anywhere.)

The staff was very pleasant and more than competent. The facility itself is most adequate. The gemsbok steak we had for dinner was outstanding.

Their equipment was all in good working order. That always makes a hunt a whole lot more fun and desirable. They also will supply guns, ammunition, fishing rods, and any equipment needed, which is certainly a plus for a beginning hunter not yet ready to make the investment needed.

For myself, they had three herds of animals that offered a great hunt: aoudad, fallow and blackbuck antelope. Since I had been looking for a good blackbuck pedestal mount to put in the office I decided to make that the animal I would go for. I felt confident this would also be a good opportunity to gather information about the Triple 777 while securing a trophy that I would be proud of.

We left the lodge and headed to the game areas. Blackbuck prefer open spaces instead of brush and wooded areas, so we headed for one of the larger areas which stretched into the open for some distance. Just as we broke through the brush and into the open, we looked off in the distance and saw a lone buck. He was too far away for a shot but as we glassed him, I was quite excited by his horns. He had **five** curls on a set of horns at least 20 or more inches.

We moved the jeep closer and he immediately took off running. We stopped and began to slip up on him. When we were about 200 yards, I decided not to try to go further.

I was using a new gun that had been built in England especially for me. It was a .270 rifle made in Winslow and Cheshire by Trevor Proctor, gunsmith to members of the royal family. Trevor had created the stock out of very beautiful French walnut. It was built on a Heimlick action which is one of the few built for left-handed action. The engraving had been done by a world renowned engraver. (I had added a little Texas flavor to it by having a drawing of Freckles, one of our ranch steers, engraved in gold on the magazine plate, along with the Clear Fork brand and my initials.)

It was a great feeling to have a gun measured and

A. M. Micallef

Record book blackbuck, taken on a crisp, sunny Texas afternoon.

fitted just for my physical characteristics, and especially for a left-handed person. Just a few days before driving to the Triple 777, I had put nine shots at 100 yards in a pattern the size of a silver dollar, so I knew it was a very accurate weapon.

I felt confident that taking this blackbuck would be a piece of cake. After hunting for game on the run in Africa, taking an antelope standing still at 200 hundred yards couldn't be a problem. That little bit of over confidence and lack of concentration resulted in one of the worst shots I've ever made.

I was aiming right above the shoulder. I think, too, I was trying to be a little bit sexy. I knew what kind of mount I wanted, so I decided to shoot as low down on the shoulders as I could so there wouldn't be any damage to the hide. That meant I was aiming low on the shoulder to begin with. Than as I squeezed off the trigger, I jerked down on the shot. I result was the bullet entered three inches below the shoulder and broke both front legs. That was definitely not a good shot.

He wouldn't run away with two broken front legs, but he certainly was suffering and thrashing around. He was not going to die without a second shot. Again, I made a mistake in not making a finishing shot immediately with my rifle. Instead, when my guide suggested that we finish the blackbuck off with his .357 magnum I tried it and made a miserable mess.

The most obvious explanation was that a pistol requires getting closer than you have to do with a rifle. The animal was already in great pain and jumping around. Trying to get close enough to get a decent shot terrorized him even more. Too, I was not only unfamiliar with this pistol, I'm not good with a pistol. After five shots I still hadn't finished him off! In frustration, I raced back to my jeep, grabbed my .270 and with one shot did what I should have done at the first.

It's a lesson simple to learn, but easy to forget, namely, a hunter should only shoot and handle weapons he is used to. That I didn't, was bad judgement on my part. A world renouned hunter, Don Corley, once told me, "Al, when you start hunting, you need to pick out two guns — a large caliber and a medium caliber —and use those for the rest of your life." He said, "Make those guns a part of you, understand them, know them, hunt them in all kinds of conditions, and it will make you a much better hunter."

It's also important to underscore that when interacting with game ranch personnel, the hunter may need to be a little more assertive when asked to do something with which he's not comfortable. That will usually make for a better hunt.

As for the animal itself, anything over 20 inches is an exceptional and respectable blackbuck antelope. This one was twenty-one and a quarter, but what really attracted me to him was he had five good, strong, well-pronounced curls, which I knew would make a very attractive trophy.

Later, I tried to analyze what had gone wrong on my first shot. For one thing, my rifle being new was part of the problem. Even though it felt great and looked even better, it was very new to me. I simply didn't have the self-confidence that comes from scores of hunts with it.

In Africa I had been shooting with a .375 and I had also shot a tremendous amount with my old .270. But guns are different. The weight is different, the feel is different and you have to get used to them. The most important thing is to gain confidence in the weapon. Once you have confidence in the weapon, and your shooting ability with that weapon, then it's a tool that you become comfortable with, and you can become very good with it.

The new rifle did cut down on my concentration. All hunters will at some time or other have a lapse of concentration. When that happens, the result will be a shot of which they're not proud. Such a shot destroys the quality and sanctity of the hunt.

Second, I had just returned from spending four weeks in Africa, three of them hunting a variety of dangerous game, as well as plains game and antelope. After taking 18 animals in three weeks, I simply couldn't call up the concentration needed for this hunt on this particular day. Shooting a small animal at that distance required even more concentration than normal.

Third, instead of pulling the trigger, I had jerked it ever so slightly. At 200 yards, a movement of an eighth of an inch can cause either a miss altogether, or only wounding.

Fourth, I needed to have gone into the woods on the right and stalked him until I was 50 or 75 yards away. Instead, because of my overconfidence and also wanting to use my new gun at a longer distance, I tried hitting him at 200 yards.

Nonetheless, it was a beautiful specimen and one I will be proud of. Its horns were wide on a relatively small bodied, very delicate looking blackbuck. This combination would make a pedestal trophy.

I had good memories of the staff and people at the Triple 777. They had done a fine job in planning and implementing the hunt I had requested. From first to last it had been a super experience and I look forward to returning.

CHAPTER XI

A "10" Exotic Big Game Hunt

There are only two kinds of hunting: good and bad. I've had both. In the process I've discovered there are a host of factors that determine a good big game hunt. I've shot record book game and felt cheated afterwards. I've downed mediocre game and felt high as a kite.

That's not true just for Texas. It can happen in Alaska, Africa, or the great Northwest. I feel fortunate to have been able to hunt in some of the finest sites in these places. And yet I must say, every time I leave the state or country to hunt, I'm always not only glad to get back to Texas, but also proud to be a part of a state which has what Texas has to offer the hunter.

There are so many advantages and opportunities to hunting in Texas that most people aren't aware of a third of them. The average hunter in the United States, or even in Texas and surrounding states, is not familiar with the intensely managed game areas in Texas. It is possible to hunt a terrific number of exotic big game in the state of Texas, and all in a very clean and challenging hunting environment.

Hunting exotic big game in Texas is also a very good way for people to get a feel for hunting exotics without traveling off to some distant part of the world that they don't understand. It provides a great training ground for becoming familiar with the right weapons, learning the habits of animals from other parts of the world, the proper conduct on safari, and learning to feel comfortable with guides, game management people and other staff.

Naturally, hunting in Texas is cheaper and safer. Foreign air travel, safari costs, import and export costs all add up. Too, with the political instability in many areas of Africa, a hunter is not always sure how safe he is at any given moment.

Equally important is the value of time. To have the variety of game resources which Texas has available within such comparatively close range is a superb **time** asset. Exotic big game can be hunted within the borders of Texas. That means only hours away, not days.

For that reason, it seems appropriate to list what for me have become the most important factors in insuring a quality exotic big game hunt in Texas. Put another way, on a scale of one to ten, what would be "A **Ten** Exotic Big Game Hunt?"

1. **The most important part of the planning for an exotic big game hunt is the environment in which the hunt is going to take place.**

The terrain in South Texas is very similar to many parts of East Africa, South Africa and Southeast Africa. Texas big game ranches are among the finest in the world, yet there is a lot of room for growth and development. That's why it's important for the hunter to be well informed about his or her expectations and be intentional about informing the game ranch in advance — before money and time are expended.

My idea of the perfect game ranch would be a ranch anywhere from 10 to 50 thousand acres that is under high fence where the animals can roam within that environment unmolested by excessive cross-fencing. In other words, they have large, unrestricted areas to roam free in. And all the animals are living in a totally integrated natural environment.

This is the most important factor in a perfect hunt for me. Obviously, there are variations that you can certainly live with, but in terms of optimum — a "10" — this is first.

2. **The second most important part of exotic big game hunting is to determine the attitude of the people who manage the game ranching operation itself.**

Most of the staff at ranches where I have hunted will provide the hunting experience that's desired. If it's a challenging fair chase hunt, most everyone is willing to do that. However, as hunters, we need to be aware that the quicker an animal is found and downed, the better it is financially for the ranch, especially for those ranches that guarantee a kill or there's no charge to the hunter.

That sometimes can result in practices that are damaging to hunting as a sport. Game ranches are businesses and they may have clientele who demand a less than sporting proposition. But it's a real turnoff to have a game rancher say to me, "We can get you anything you want to hunt or want to shoot." What they mean is they know someone who has a particular animal for sale which the rancher will buy and transport to his ranch. Then when the hunter arrives he will hunt for it as though it was born on that ranch.

It's been my experience that those kinds of people are the exception and not the rule in Texas. Fortunately, there are people who will always do their very best to make a hunt the most authentic hunting experience to be had. They make hunting the good sport it is.

3. **The third most important thing to decide upon is the kind of hunting experience wanted.**

One of the decisions that has to be made is whether to hunt for trophies or to hunt for the **experience** of trophy hunting. Those two don't necessarily go hand-in-hand. Hunting for big trophies in a fair chase hunt is very difficult and challenging, but it can be done. To me, it's the best. But as any hunter knows, finding **the** trophy animal is not a sure thing. Four to five hundred yards away, one aoudad with 29 inch horns looks almost identical to one 31 inches long. After spending a half day stalking an animal, it's not unusual to discover that he's not the right one, after all. But if the hunting experience itself is the goal, then no one feels cheated; and if the trophy animal was taken, well and good.

4. **The fourth most important thing is to give adequate time for the kind of hunting desired.**

One of the beauties of exotic big game hunting in Texas is the availability of almost any kind of hunting wanted. However, each takes different amounts of time to complete. It's possible to get in a truck, get close to the animal wanted and fire from the window. This can be accomplished many times in a half day or less. Or it's possible to combine safari hunting in a vehicle with stalking on foot. That can be done in a day with luck. But to have an adequate amount of time for a fair chase hunt may require a minimum of two to three days for most wild game.

But the choice is the hunter's.

5. **The next most important thing in exotic big game hunting is the guide.**

Some of the best guides in the world are right here in Texas. They would match up with any guide in Alaska or Africa. But there are also some for whom guiding is driving a truck until they spot some game, stopping the truck and getting out and taking a shot.

The best guides in Texas would have to include Finn Aagaard, a Professional White Hunter from Kenya, and Bryan Coleman, also a PH from Kenya. These men have a reservoir of experience and training that is simply not available to us in America. The rigorous standards and the years of apprenticeship required before they could belong to a Professional Hunting Association is most impressive. Another guide who has always given me a great hunt would have to be Uncle Warren at the YO. Some of the most memorable hunting experiences I've had have been with him. He's not only a class individual but a fine hunter with a world of experience behind him.

In addition to their hunting savvy, guides need to be expert and skilled at field dressing and at keeping and handling the cape in a manner that will deliver to the hunter the best possible trophy. That means having affiliations with the proper meat processors and taxidermists to insure a quality product.

Though it's probably light years away, what is needed in Texas exotic big game hunting are professional standards for guides which would insure not only a minimum of competence and training, but also commitment to certain ethics of hunting that the industry could count on. In other parts of the world, I'm always much more comfortable hunting with a guide whom I know is a member of a professional hunting association. It means he has pledged himself to those high standards of hunting.

6. **Next in importance is the game available.**

Some ranches have developed strong herds of particular animals. Usually, these have been stocked on the ranch for many years. These are the ones that will provide the best hunt. Some inquiry of the managers at these ranches will usually divulge the information needed. Too, if you're interested in trophy book animals, an examination of the trophy animals previously taken will give a good indication of what to expect.

That would also mean hunting animals that have been raised on the ranching operation itself. Naturally, it will be difficult for the new game ranches. And we all have to face the realities of the economics of any venture. But ideally, there needs to be time enough for the animals on the ranch to birth their replacements, rather than their having been bought from a wholesaler or game broker for harvesting the next hunting season. Or even worse, purchased the week before or the day before just for you.

This also underscores the need of game management. Too many animals on one ranch is extremely destructive. Since most game ranches have six to eight foot fences, the animals cannot naturally move to less populated areas when overcrowding occurs. For exotics that's devastating. The stress that results will mean more susceptibility to disease and parasites, less ability to withstand temperature extremes, and in the worst of cases, starvation.

One of the ways most ranches attempt to solve their overpopulation problems is to provide supplemental feeding. But more important is to recognize certain census maximums above which a herd will not be allowed to go. For example, I was impressed with the policy at the Flying A; when their blackbuck population grew too large, to reduce it they slashed their prices to hardly a third of what other ranches were charging.

7. **Also important are the lodge and staff environment.**

A hunter wants to associate with people who enjoy hunting, and who have had excellent hunting experience. That not only insures an informed hunt, it also means being with people easy to relate to and talk with. Given the cost of these hunts — although they are certainly less expensive than traveling around the world hunting — it's not unreasonable to expect accommodations that are clean, well maintained, good food and a courteous and responsive staff.

Though this will not affect the size of the trophy to be hunted, it is significant. I always look forward to eating at the YO; and I still remember the incredible sophistication of the meals at the Aagaards in what were very simple quarters.

These seven points do not exhaust the prerequisites of a a good hunt, but in my opinion they are some of the most important. Once the criteria have been set and agreed upon, it's important to stick to them and not be coaxed into doing something different. While that may not necessarily guarantee a perfect hunt, it should mean a fun hunt and a quality hunting experience.

CHAPTER XII

The Original Texas Exotics

In the early 1930's, some farsighted visionaries imported six species of animals into Texas. These six were: aoudad sheep, mouflon sheep, sika deer, fallow deer, axis deer, and blackbuck antelope. Combined, they offer animal beauty, beautiful hides and coats, magnificent antlers and horns, and some of the finest hunting anywhere in the world.

Until Tommy Thompson incorporated the name for his company, these six were referred to as the "Texotics;" they're now referred to as "common" exotics. They were particularly adaptable to Hill Country climate and have proved the wisdom of their original importers.

William Reaves, Lonestar Photography

Aoudads at rest. But notice that they are always alert!

Aoudad

("Barbary Sheep")

The aoudad is the ultimate in exotic game hunting. I have hunted animals all over the world, and except for the absence of the danger factor, aoudad hunting can be as challenging as any hunting anywhere.

There are several reasons for this. First, is their eyesight: it's incredible. They seem to have telescopic lens giving them the ability to spot the slightest movement at a mile or more. Their hearing is equally sensitive. They are very wary of humans and move very quickly. I've never known them to stand around and allow time to take aim. Also, their coats seem to match the rough areas in which they flourish: cliffy, rocky areas, full of bush and brush. Nearly always, the view will be limited to the upper back or shoulders and seldom a good frontal view for a lung and heart hit. That means the shots will be either at a long distance or at a moving target. It makes trophy hunting very difficult, indeed.

This magnificent animal would now be extinct had it not been brought from North Africa to American zoos in the early 1900's. It has done very well in captivity. As with so many African animals, it has become extinct in its former Sahara homeland due to excessive poaching. In the 1950's, several large herds were released into the Hill Country, Brewster County in West Texas and in the Palo Dura Canyon area of the Texas Panhandle. The rough and rugged terrain of these areas has been perfect for the aoudad. In every respect, they have become acclimated.

Strangely, it reproduces with domestic goats but not with domestic sheep. Though it's technically known as a sheep its name, "aoudad," means "sand goat." Whether a sheep (sometimes referred to as "Barbary Sheep") or goat, it's an outstanding specimen.

Its color is a rich light brown. It has leggings or chaps of long hair that hang over the forelegs with a mane extending from the front of the neck and down the throat to the brisket.

The aoudad ram weighs around 300 pounds. Their hindquarters are smaller than the forequarters. When combined with the pronounced chaps in the front, that makes it appear to be all chest, which is one reason why they are such a beautiful half life size mount.

A big set of aoudad horns are a trophy hunter's dream. They start up at the top and then sweep around and down in at the tips. I've heard of 36 inch horns, but never been able to land one. While hunting at Valdena Farms in Utopia, I had one in my scope that would have been close to that but I hit a small tree limb that scattered the bullet. I have several stunning life size half mounts, the biggest of which has 29½ inch horns. In addition to the length, these horns are massive in circumference and can measure up to 12 inches.

The problem in hunting for a trophy ram is that because of their extremely acute hearing and vision it's difficult to get close. And even when 100 yards away, (and getting that close is a rarity which I've only been able to do with the aid of Professional White Hunter,

Bryan Coleman) it's difficult to know for sure whether you have a potential record setter or a typical trophy.

That's when other factors such as the coat and color have to be taken into consideration. In old rams, their chaps stand out much more distinctly and appear to be darker and richer.

Their patterns help some. Aoudads usually run in herds patterned along gender lines. The biggest herds will be females and their young and yearlings. Young rams tend to leave the herd as yearlings and run in bachelor groups. Old trophy rams occasionally can be seen with a female herd, but more often than not with other older rams. During the rutting season though, rams of all ages will be near the ewe herds. Fighting among the rams is constant and serious and continues until all the ewes are settled.

Dr. Burkett has said of this animal, "Aoudad sheep hunting in North America is perhaps the finest hunting opportunity on the continent in terms of both trophy quality and sport." That's a statement with which I would heartily concur.

I've hunted and tracked these animals for hours and finally seen only one or two, I thought. Then they would either sense me or another animal like the Sika would give an alert. Suddenly, what I thought was one or two would become a whole herd; the entire hillside would seem to move. Their coats had given them superb camouflage.

The meat on an aoudad is not what I would call a gourmet's delight. I've tasted it, and it is something that I wouldn't mind avoiding.

Chuck Gordon

Mouflon Sheep
BURKETT TROPHY GAME RECORDS OF THE WORLD
Registered in the name of A. M. Micallef, Registration No. 2360. Currently ranks 22nd in the world, and is a Class B trophy in the Modern Arm Division. (8-27-84)

Mouflon Sheep

The mouflon sheep hails from Corsica in the Mediterranean. It's the smallest of the world's wild sheep.

Unless mouflon are hunted in a wild state and environment, they are probably the easiest hunt of all the exotics. I hunted mouflon sheep with Professional White Hunter, Finn Aagaard, in Llano, Texas, and it turned out to be a very challenging hunt. It was helped by their having roamed free for many years, without supplemental feeding, on thousands of acres and truly rugged terrain. In very hilly country, with rock outcroppings and cliff faces, mouflon can be a hunt that will match almost any other wild sheep. But if they are in big, open pastures, on relatively flat land with some rolling hills, they can be an easy and disappointing hunt.

They make beautiful mounted trophies. Their horns are among the most impressive of any exotics. They start out to the side and then gradually curl in to the face right below the eye.

The coloration on a mouflon is exceptional. A true mouflon will mix black and white on a fawn or white colored saddle patch that makes an excellent trophy. It has a brown or sandy red back and black mane with a black and brown face. This combined with its long hair combine to give the mouflon a striking appearance.

I've eaten mouflon in stews and prepared in various other ways. Finn Aagaard's wife, Berit, cooked one of the finest tasting meat dishes I've ever had anywhere and it was mouflon. Although mouflon get bad press, they can be an exceptional dining experience.

One of the problems in hunting for trophy mouflon is the crossbreeding that's taken place with other sheep. Knowing the purity of the breed is especially difficult when hunting in the wild.

Nonetheless, mouflon sheep can be an excellent hunt, especially for the first time hunter or young person.

William Reaves, Lonestar Photography

Fallow

Fallow Deer

I've been told that George Washington was the first American to import fallow deer to America. The fallow comes from the Mediterranean region of Europe and is best known as the "European fallow." They have adjusted well and can now be found in many states of the Union. They were first brought into Texas in the early 1930's.

Fallow deer are very fascinating from the standpoint that there are really three basic fallows (plus some interesting color variations of these): a white fallow, that at the right time of the year is snow white; a spotted fallow, which is a white-wheat color with big, large white spots; and the brown or chocolate fallow.

Though it depends on how heavily a particular game ranch has been hunted, the best antlers will be on bucks that are between six and nine years of age. During rut, bucks will be seen with does, but once the does are settled, the buck will run pretty much on his own.

In hunting challenge, they are about the same as an axis, although, I believe that they can be more illusive than an axis. They don't have quite the curiosity of an axis. Most axis will run off, stop and look back. Fallow don't seem to have that habit. They will lay those big palmed antlers back, point that nose, and keep on moving through the brush. Surprisingly, they move quickly through very dense foliage.

They also are easily domesticated which makes them an ideal choice for new game ranches. They can be moved around much more easily than some of the other exotics in Texas.

A fully grown buck will be about three feet at the shoulders and weigh between 150 and 200 pounds. As far as the edibility of the meat of a fallow, I've been told by many guides that the meat is not a really good game meat. However, I have had some fallow back strap which I thought was certainly acceptable. And though it was not the same as axis, I have had good fallow steaks. Still, none of it is the same quality that you might get in an axis or in a blackbuck antelope. But as long as the animal was not taken in rut, it's good enough. Meat taken in rut will normally have a very gamey flavor.

Fallow are not that great a hide. Sometimes a good spotted fallow is okay, but the white fallow and chocolate brown fallow are not really that acceptable as rugs; however they do make good looking shoulder mounts. I've been told that fallow are very susceptible to tick infestation which downgrades the quality of their hide. For certain a fallow taken during rut will have an unacceptable hide due to the habit of bucks to urinate on themselves during rut. The effect of the urine on the hide damages both the color and the hair.

Sika

William Reaves, Lonestar Photography

Sika Deer

Three of the thirteen varieties of the sika deer are widely available for hunting in Texas: the Japanese sika, the Formosan sika and the Manchurian sika. These animals are small bodied, fine horned and very similar to a reindeer in horn structure. A few Dybowski sika are also being slowly introduced; these have a much longer and heavier horn than the other sika and make an outstanding trophy.

The Japanese sika is the smallest of the sika. It's around 30 inches at the shoulders and will average in excess of 100 pounds. It has a different coat in the spring and summer from that of the fall and winter. During the warmer months, it's brown with white spots; in the cooler months, the spots disappear and the coat turns darker. Since they can sometimes be confused with other deer, one of the distinguishing characteristics of all sika is a patch of white encircling their tail.

The Formosan sika is much larger than its Japanese relatives. Big males will measure three feet at the shoulders and weigh from 150 to 180 pounds. They too have a change in the color of their coats between warm and cold weather. Their summer coat is spotted chestnut; the winter coat turns dark brown and the spots are much more difficult to detect. They also have the white patch on their rump.

The Manchurian sika is the second largest of all sika. Mature bucks will reach up to 40 inches high and weigh between 200 and 250 pounds. Their coat tends to match the Formosan sika in terms of seasonal changes.

Dybowski sika is the largest of all the sika. I saw several of these on the Triple 777 ranch in Hondo, though they were not yet ready for hunting. They stood more than 43 inches at the shoulders and weighed between 250 and 300 pounds.

The sika has been called the watchdog of the forest; when alarmed they make a sound like a barking dog. Many's the time that I've been tracking another animal and a sika would spot me and begin barking like a watchdog. Needless to say, I could say goodbye to the quarry I was tracking.

As to hunting the sika, it is a fairly curious animal and in some environments is a relatively easy hunt. This is especially true if they are fed supplemental feed. However, they are very wary and smart animals.

I've found that even though a first impression in scouting a ranch may be one of large numbers of game standing around which would be easy to harvest, that picture changes drastically when stalking begins. Once a hunter leaves his vehicle and starts moving around, they can be gone like a flash.

Although a sika can be a relatively easy hunt, finding a quality trophy is fairly difficult. The old males in any breed are very difficult to hunt. This greatly enhances the challenge of the hunt.

The meat of a sika is pretty reasonable venison. Again, it doesn't compare to the axis, but it certainly is palatable and good.

William Reaves, Lonestar Photography

Blackbuck Antelope

Blackbuck Antelope

The blackbuck is an absolutely incredible and beautiful animal and one of my favorite trophies. On a scale of one to ten, it hunts in the seven to nine range and occasionally gets a ten depending on the hunting environment. Part of this is due to the incredible speed of the blackbuck. It supposedly ranks second only to the Cheetah, and sometimes reaches speeds of 55 mph. In a big and open area that's not brushy, they will start running a quarter of a mile away from you. The adult bucks who have the beautiful "V" shaped, ringed or corkscrew spiral horns are very wary of hunters or any movement. They can be an exceptional hunt.

The "masked bandit" look provides a head and shoulder mount that is absolutely beautiful. And of course, a blackbuck rug or hanging, with its black and white fawn colored hide is to be cherished.

The blackbuck comes from the plains of India. Our American herds are thought to have originated in what is now Pakistan. The number of blackbuck in Texas is thought to be among the largest in the world, possibly surpassing the number in their homeland.

A grown male will weigh around 100 pounds. Only males have horns. A grown buck of three years age will have horns that measure between 15 to 18 inches in length. And although a male reaches his prime at approximately six years of age, it's rare to see horns that exceed 20 inches. Part of the reason for this is that blackbucks never shed. Consequently, their horns are liable to be damaged in fights and territorial acts. Now and then a trophy horn will exceed 20 inches. The only place I've seen that is at Onion Creek, near Austin. Whether it's the weather or the environment, no Texas blackbuck has ever equalled the world record 32 inch blackbuck from India.

Blackbucks can be hunted year round. Good sized herds can be found in south Texas and the Hill Country. They seem to prefer open grazing areas as opposed to the shrubs and bush of many animals. Rather than using their coat for camouflage, they seem to prefer the open area where they can use their speed.

Their unique social organization has been documented in a fascinating study done at the Greenwood Valley Ranch by a doctoral candidate. "Territorial males" establish an area in which they group from three to eight does. The does will stay within this territory for a limited time. After birthing their babies they cycle for breeding at least once a week until settled. Their babies tend to match up, or twin, with another baby.

Blackbuck meat is excellent. It's lean and dark and when prepared properly it is very tender and has little of the "game" taste that some wild animals have.

The blackbuck's coat darkens as he ages. Social

status, along with the time of the year and the age of the buck, influence color. The bucks who stay the darkest in the summer are usually territorial bucks. And in the unique social ranking of this species, high ranking bucks may begin to blacken as early as their yearling year.

William Reaves, Lonestar Photography

Axis doe and fawn.

William Reaves, Lonestar Photography

Axis buck.

Axis Deer

Of all the exotic big game in Texas, there's none I value more highly than the axis deer. Though beauty is in the eye of the beholder, I've always felt the axis combines the best of everything. Its adaptability to the environment, its fertility, its beauty and the quality of its meat make it the number one import of every exotic big game ranch.

The axis was first imported from India to Texas in the 1930's. It's been a popular addition to Texas wild life ever since and has multiplied rapidly. Estimates range from 25,000 up. The number "free-ranging" is in the thousands.

Their rapid growth and adaptability has caused some concern that they would crowd out the white-tailed deer populaton. In fact, many feel that it is already the second most important game animal in Texas.

The axis has a beautiful reddish brown coat with small white spots dotting it. Its eyes are dark and almond-shaped. A dark line runs down the back from the head all the way to the tail. Its throat is white as is most of its stomach and the inside of the legs.

An axis coat stays the same color throughout the year. Tanned, it makes excellent leather coats and vests, and a full hide is beautiful on the wall or floor.

A grown buck will stand around three feet at the shoulders and weigh between 175 and 200 pounds on the hoof. Field dressed he will go at around 15 pounds.

Like most of the deer family, axis have great eye sight. This makes them hard to approach without being seen. Added to this defense is excellent hearing and a well-developed sense of smell.

Their antlers are plain in design, but incredibly large for their body size. They will range somewhere between 25 to 30 inches. Anything over 25 is outstanding.

Since female axis can conceive at any time of year, it's difficult to date their rut. However, most breeding occurs in the late spring.

One of the best things about an axis is the outstanding quality of its meat. It is seldom gamey, even from an old buck. It's lean and tender and far superior to the beef steaks at the store.

I have several axis trophies. The one I'm proudest of has brow-line 32 inches long and measures 31 across.

SUPER-EXOTICS

One of the obvious distinctions to be made about the super exotics is that they are much more rare, usually, much larger animals, and consequently, more costly to hunt. For that reason, they do not seem to me to be as important as the basic six written about above. Yet, there are some enterprising game ranches in Texas which are beginning to stock a fascinating variety of super exotics. Those listed below are the three I've found to be most available.

ELAND

My hunting experience with eland has all been in Africa in a ranch environment, but a very large ranching operation with no cross-fencing. This ranch of more than 150 thousand acres had a veldt much like the open and rolling plains of Texas.

To find an eland in the veldt, it's necessary to climb to its highest point and then spend several hours glassing. Once found then it's a very long stalk to get into position.

Eland are the largest of the antelope family. They're a massive and beautiful beast, with bulls weighing as much as 2,000 pounds. The bull elands that I've seen in Texas were comparable to those in Africa.

Most of the elands in Texas were originally brought in by the YO in the 1950's. They continue to have a sizeable herd.

I have had eland steak before and found it to be some of the best game meat available. One of the drawbacks to hunting the eland is the cost. Most ranches will charge from $4,000 up for a bull eland.

William Reaves, Lonestar Photography

Gemsbok

GEMSBOK

Gemsbok are very beautiful. In open terrain they can be a very challenging animal to hunt. They are very wary of humans or human movement and are extremely fast. Once alerted they are almost impossible to chase.

The gemsbok has been established in Texas for a long time and was first brought into Texas by the YO in the 1950's. Like the oryx, they require minimal water and minerals. They have beautiful hides and are a marvelous trophy mount.

While hunting at the Triple 777, they served some excellent gemsbok steaks. Others have reported similar positive responses to the meat of this animal.

William Reaves, Lonestar Photography

Scimitar-horned Oryx

SCIMITAR-HORNED ORYX

It's quite surprising, but there is a substantial population of scimitar-horned oryx in Texas. In fact, the hunting for scimitar-horned oryx in Texas is better than it is in Africa. Though there may be some limited exceptions, I'm unaware of any area in North Africa where they can be hunted legally.

That means to hunt a scimitar-horned oryx, especially a trophy oryx, Texas is the place to do it.

The scimitar-horned oryx is one of the largest of the antelopes of North Africa and is closely related to the gemsbok of Southern Africa. They were brought to America about 25 years ago and have successfully reproduced ever since.

In my opinion, the oryx is a unique trophy and one to be prized. The trophy oryx I shot at the YO had horns exceeding 45 inches. The average is around 40 inches. They make a magnificent trophy. In addition, I make a rug out of the hide.

The oryx is dominantly white or cream with several patterns of orange and brown over its body. The neck is orange or rust colored with a brown strip around the legs and eyes. Its body is not as sleek as some antelope and deer, but it is a unique and beautiful animal nonetheless. And because of its conditioning in North Africa, it is able to withstand erratic temperature changes as well as extremely long periods without water.

Since it is a night browser, it is difficult to find during the day, unless it has become used to certain salt or mineral licks.

Surprisingly, the oryx is excellent meat. It is much like its larger cousin, the eland, in being some of the most prized of the antelope family.

A. M. Micallef

Splendid nine foot brown bear. On my right, Jim Brannam, guide.

CHAPTER XIII

Texas Whitetail and Alaskan Brown Bear

In late October, I contracted with outfitter Jim Brannam in Alaska for a brown bear hunt. I had scheduled nine days for the hunt. Our first day out we went to Ursus Cove on the Aleutian Penninsula. The weather was hovering around freezing with winds of 40 to 60 miles per hour roaring in off of the Bering Sea.

The first day out we had traveled ten miles or more in hip waders in misting rain and snow, when we spotted a brown bear at the timber line in a blueberry patch. We spent an hour maneuvering to get downwind of him by following a stream through some waterfalls and then over a rise to a ravine. We crawled to the edge of the ravine hoping he would still be there.

Fortunately, he was, but when I took aim my scope had iced over, even though I had it covered. My first shot broke both shoulders. I took what I thought were seven more well placed shots with my .375 H & H Holland, using a 300 grain soft point bullet.

It then took us ten minutes to get to where he had fallen over. Just as we got there, he pushed up on his legs and gave the most blood curdling scream I've ever heard. I took one more shot that broke his spine and he fell over dead.

When we skinned him out, we confirmed that seven of my shots had been in the heart and lungs, one in the spine and a bad one which had hit in the stomach. We skinned him, packed his skin and skull, and headed in.

Murphy's Law was at work again. I had found a great bear my first day out. After a couple of days of visiting with other hunters and making some business contacts, I left early and headed back to Texas. Once there, I decided it was a good time to go to the YO and hunt some more.

Alaska and Texas: the two biggest states in the Union, and great hunting places as well.

The Hill Country of Texas has more whitetail deer than any place in the world. In fact, in Llano County alone, from 10 to 15 thousand whitetail are taken each fall during the hunting season. Immediately following, whitetail can still be seen hopping fences and browsing in pastures all over the territory.

The YO has a contest each year for the biggest whitetail taken from either the YO itself or the many whitetail leases they maintain. The winner receives a YO rifle that a lot of people really prize. I hadn't hunted whitetail that much, but I decided I would go for the prize.

I arrived at the YO in the afternoon and met up with my favorite guide, Uncle Warren. On the way in, Uncle Warren had met a couple of people who were vacationing from Seattle. They had somehow stumbled into the YO and wanted to take a tour of the ranch. Normally, tours are available. But on this particular day, due to the heavy number of hunters, there was no one available to lead the tour.

Uncle Warren introduced me to the couple, a retired lady and gentleman who had never seen a Texas ranch before, nor one with Longhorn cattle, and for certain not one with a hunting program on it.

Uncle Warren is the epitome of southern courtesy. He asked me privately if I would mind if this couple rode along with my daughter, Amanda, and me. (My son, Michael, had gone on so many hunting trips with me that Amanda had insisted it was her turn.) I visited with the couple briefly. I asked them if they had ever hunted or been involved with hunting at all, and they said no. I thought that might be a problem, but since Uncle Warren had made the request, I agreed.

We spent the afternoon combing the different ranch areas where Uncle Warren felt there would be record book whitetail. Toward evening, in the 10,000 acre Live Oak range, we spotted a beautiful eight pointer with tines that looked as though they would measure 5 to 6

A. M. Micallef

Whitetail deer. My smiling daughter, Amanda, on my right.

inches, with a spread of about 22 inches. He was about 200 yards away with his head sticking around some scrub oak. He was an incredibly beautiful animal. When we stopped the vehicle he immediately ran about two to three hundred yards away and stopped to look back at us.

Uncle Warren was confident that if we could stay under cover where the whitetail couldn't see us, with the wind blowing at his back toward us, so he couldn't smell us, we might be able to get close enough for a better shot.

So we left Amanda and the vacationers in the car, and Uncle Warren and I started slowly on our hands and knees, moving from bush to bush. We kept going to the left keeping the wind to our back. The deer relaxed and started to graze. We caught a glimpse of him and could tell that he didn't seem to be alarmed. We kept moving until we were about 175 yards from him with his back end facing us. Just then, two axis saw us, and darted past him. He raised his head and ran off about ten yards, then he turned to look back at us. I raised my rifle and caught him in the sight just as he was about to run off. He dropped instantly. By the time we reached him, he was dead.

The people who were with us had been able to see the whole thing: the animal, our stalking, and the shot. That was a memorable hunt. And the prize rifle? We were in the top five, but not the winners. As they used to say in Brooklyn, "Wait until next year!" (In 1984, the prize was a set of binoculars. We won with a nineteen point extra-typical buck.)

CHAPTER XIV

Taxidermy and Field Care

by Neal Coldwell
Woodbury Taxidermy in Kerrville, Texas

The high prices charged for game animal hunting these days means extra care should be taken in choosing an outfitter and taxidermist. Good taxidermy begins with the hunter in the field **before** the taxidermist is ever involved. Proper field care is essential to proper mounting of a trophy animal. For that to happen, I recommend that hunters go to their taxidermists before their hunting trip for a few tips regarding the field care of their mount.

For example, as soon as the animal is killed it should be field dressed. The removal of the bowels and vital organs immediately upon killing is essential. This is especially true if the meat of the animal is going to be eaten; and it is also important to a quality mounting and hide.

After field dressing, if you are near your taxidermist, take it to him for skinning. If you are not near a taxidermy shop, here are some important considerations for skinning your animal:

1. Begin by cutting directly down the middle of the back and making a circular cut around the body of the animal behind the shoulder. Always cut behind the shoulder to insure that there is an adequate amount of hide for a full shoulder mount.

2. After making a cut behind the shoulder, make a cut behind each of the front legs and then "V" the cut back to your circular cut. Always save all the hide off the brisket of your animal. **Do not cut the throat**.

3. After skinning the hide down to the last neck vertebrae, cut the skull and hide loose from the body. Then roll the hide (flesh side in) to the head.

4. If it will be some time before the head and hide can be taken to the taxidermist, they should be frozen.

A hunter should get to know his taxidermist well. As in any business or service, some are better than others. In determining which taxidermist to use, a hunter should look at their display mounts very closely. The mounts should look lifelike. The noses of the mounts should not be filled with wax. They should have depth to them. The eyes should be clear with no paint or wax on them. The hide should fit around the horns tightly. The hide down the back of the animal should be sewn together tightly so that no stitches are showing. Neither the hide nor the ears should have cracked areas.

It's also important to determine if the taxidermist has the hides professionally tanned. The tanning process takes much longer than mounting, and it is absolutely necessary to keep the hide and ears from cracking. A tanned hide is just like leather and therefore the lifetime of the mount is extended considerably by tanning.

A big concern of all hunters is how soon they can get their mount back. Though that's understandable, the length of time taken in preparing a mount should not influence the choosing of a taxidermist. Eight to ten months is a reasonable period of time for a quality mount to be completed.

The price of the finished trophy should not be a factor in the decision either. A mount which costs $300 but is preserved properly and lasts a lifetime averages out at very little per year. On the other hand, a mount which costs $240 and lasts only three years before deteriorating would cost $80 per year.

When the taxidermist receives your mount the first thing he does is to skin the hide off the head. The ears are then turned inside out, the lips and eyelids are slit, and all the meat is removed. The thick parts of the hide, particularly on the back of the neck, are thinned down by removing part of the skin. This is done to prevent hair slippage. The flesh side of the hide is salted very well with a finely granulated mixing salt. The salt dries and holds the hair until the hide is tanned. After drying, the hide is sent to the tannery.

Once the tanning process is finished and the hide is returned, the taxidermist places it in a mild tanning solution to soften it. All holes are then repaired and the hide is ready to be mounted. The horns are set upon a papier mache form that matches the size and style of the mount requested. (For this process to be maximally effective two things are very helpful: one, is a closeup picture of the animal from the front and side; second, a neck measurement behind the jaw and the middle of the neck is very helpful in recreating the proper size of the animal.)

The next step is setting the eyes and modeling the nose and mouth with modeling clay. This is an important part of a quality mount. It depends upon the taxidermist's ability as an artist to use clay to recreate the lifelike look of the animal. Glue is then put on the form and hide is slipped over it. After the hide is tucked around the nose and mouth, then the eyes and the ears are set. Finally, the hide is sewn down the back.

Upon completing the sewing, the hide is styled to a backboard. The mounted animal is now ready for finishing. Finishing the mount includes painting the nose, ears, and eyes plus adding other touches that are needed.

Though the above is a very brief description of taxidermy and the field care of an animal, hopefully, it will help in the choosing of a quality taxidermist. Please feel free to stop by Woodbury Taxidermy the next time you're in Kerrville. We would be glad to assist you in any way possible with your taxidermy needs.

A. M. Micallef

Axis

BURKETT TROPHY GAME RECORDS OF THE WORLD.
Registered in the name of A. M. Micallef, Registration No. 2357. Currently ranks 95th in the world and is a Class B Trophy in the Modern Arm Division. (8/27/84)

Aoudad

Trophy Aoudad pictured with my wife, Jane.

BURKETT TROPHY GAME RECORDS OF THE WORLD.

Registered in the name of A. M. Micallef, Registration No. 2326. Currently ranks 49th in the world and is a Class B Trophy in the Modern Arm Division. (4/25/84) Score 325.5

Chuck Gordon

Axis

BURKETT TROPHY GAME RECORDS OF THE WORLD.

Registered in the name of A. M. Micallef, Registration No. 2200. Currently ranks 89th in the world and is a Class B Trophy in the Modern Arm Division. (6/15/83)

Chuck Gordon

Axis
BURKETT TROPHY GAME RECORDS OF THE WORLD.
Registered in the name of Mike Micallef, Registration No. 2232. Currently ranks 93rd in the world and is a Class B Trophy in the Modern Arm Division. (9/24/83) Score 301.6

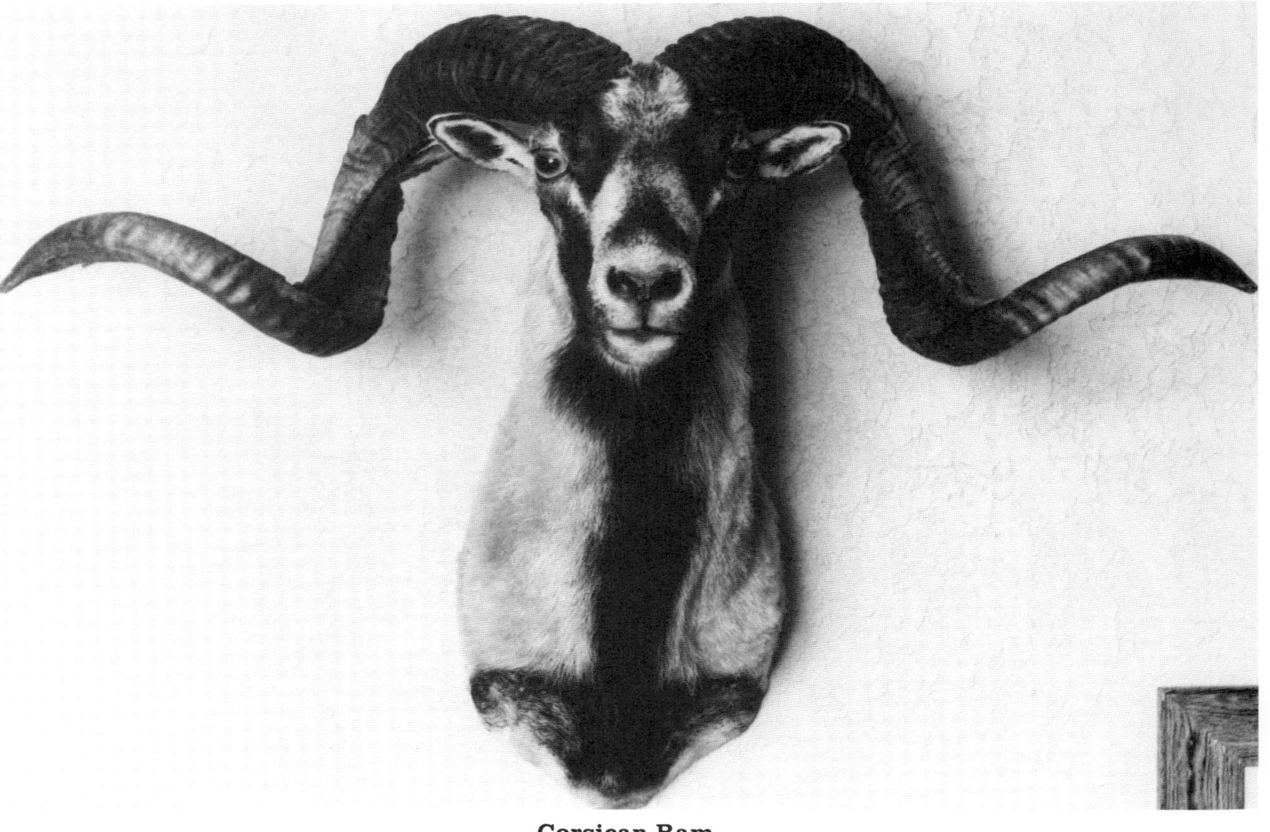

Chuck Gordon

Corsican Ram
BURKETT TROPHY GAME RECORDS OF THE WORLD.
Registered in the name of A. M. Micallef, Registration No. 2256. Currently ranks 32nd in the world and is a Class A Trophy in the Modern Arm Division. (9/24/83) Score 303.3

Blackbuck Antelope
BURKETT TROPHY GAME RECORDS OF THE WORLD.
Registered in the name of A. M. Micallef, Registration No. 2382. Third Place Award 1980-1984. Currently ranks 7th in the world and is a Record Class Trophy in the Modern Arm Division. (4/25/84) Score 235.7

Chuck Gordon

Fallow Deer

BURKETT TROPHY GAME RECORDS OF THE WORLD.
Registered in the name of A. M. Micallef, Registration No. 2382. Currently ranks 13th in the world and is a Class A Trophy in the Modern Arm Division. (1/22/85)

Brown Ibex

BURKETT TROPHY GAME RECORDS OF THE WORLD.

Registered in the name of A. M. Micallef, Registration No. 2260. Currently ranks 12th in the world and is a Class B Trophy in the Modern Arm Division. (9/24/83) Score 270.3

Chuck Gordon

Iranian White Ibex

BURKETT TROPHY GAME RECORDS OF THE WORLD.

Registered in the name of A. M. Micallef, Registration No. 2259. First Place Award 1980-1984. Currently ranks 4th in the world and is a Class A Trophy in the Modern Arm Division. (9/24/83) Score 307.5

A. M. Micallef

Scimitar-horned Oryx
BURKETT TROPHY GAME RECORDS OF THE WORLD.
Registered in the name of A. M. Micallef, Registration No. 2359. First place Award for 1980-1984. Currently ranks 2nd in the world and is a Record Class Trophy in the Modern Arm Division. (8/27/84) Score 294.2

Chuck Gordon

Sika

BURKETT TROPHY GAME RECORDS OF THE WORLD.

Registered in the name of A. M. Micallef, Registration No. 2336. Currently ranks 42nd in the world and is a Class C Trophy in the Modern Arm Division. (9/24/83) Score 214.7

Chuck Gordon

Catalina Goat

BURKETT TROPHY GAME RECORDS OF THE WORLD.

Registered in the name of Michael A. Micallef, Registration No. 2254. Currently ranks 18th in the world and is a Class A Trophy in the Modern Arm Division. (9/24/83)

Chuck Gordon

SAFARI CLUB INTERNATIONAL
Record-book Gemsbok

Chuck Gordon

SAFARI CLUB INTERNATIONAL
Record-book Bushbuck

Chuck Gordon

SAFARI CLUB INTERNATIONAL
Record-book Blesbok

Chuck Gordon

SAFARI CLUB INTERNATIONAL
Record-book Waterbuck

Chuck Gordon

Impala (left)
SAFARI CLUB INTERNATIONAL
Record-book Eland (right)

Chuck Gordon

SAFARI CLUB INTERNATIONAL
Record-book Hartebeest

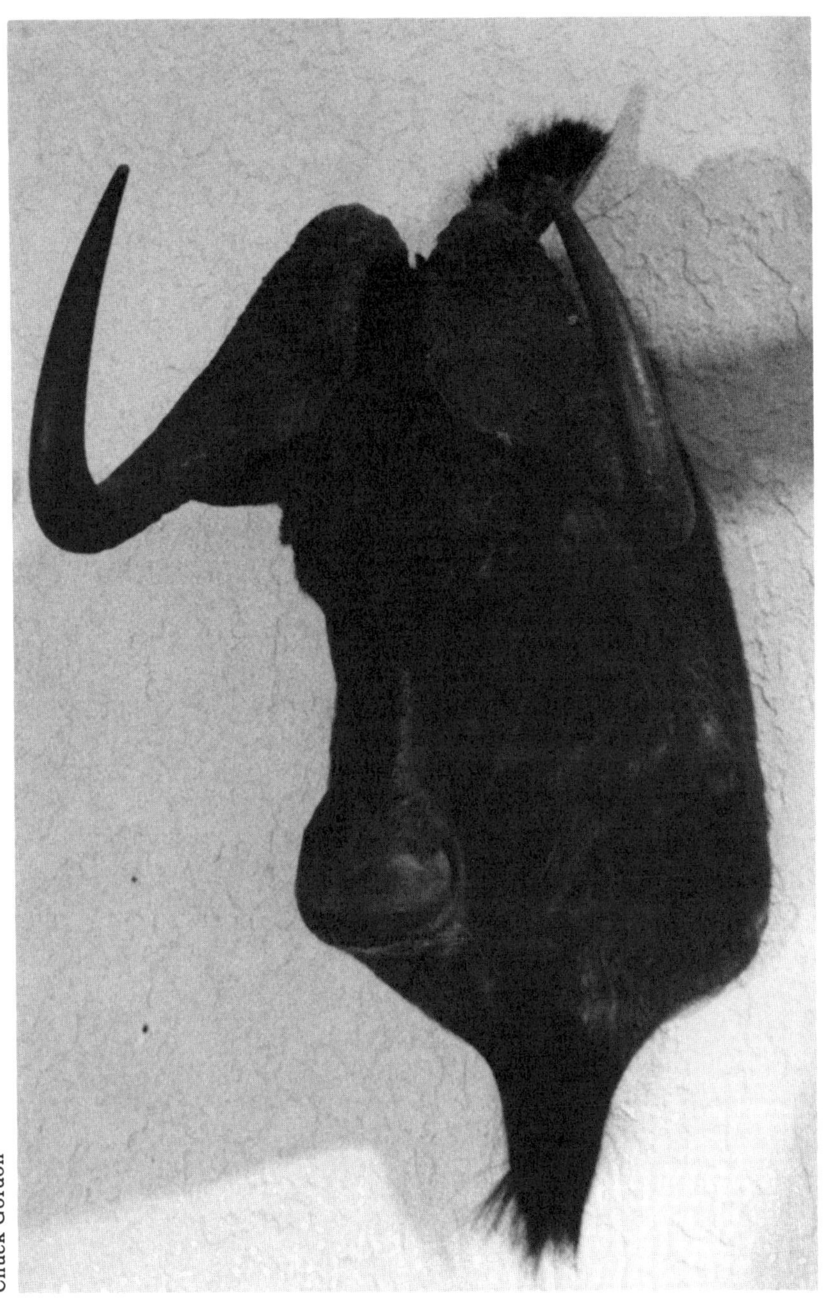
Chuck Gordon

White-tailed Neu

Texas Dall

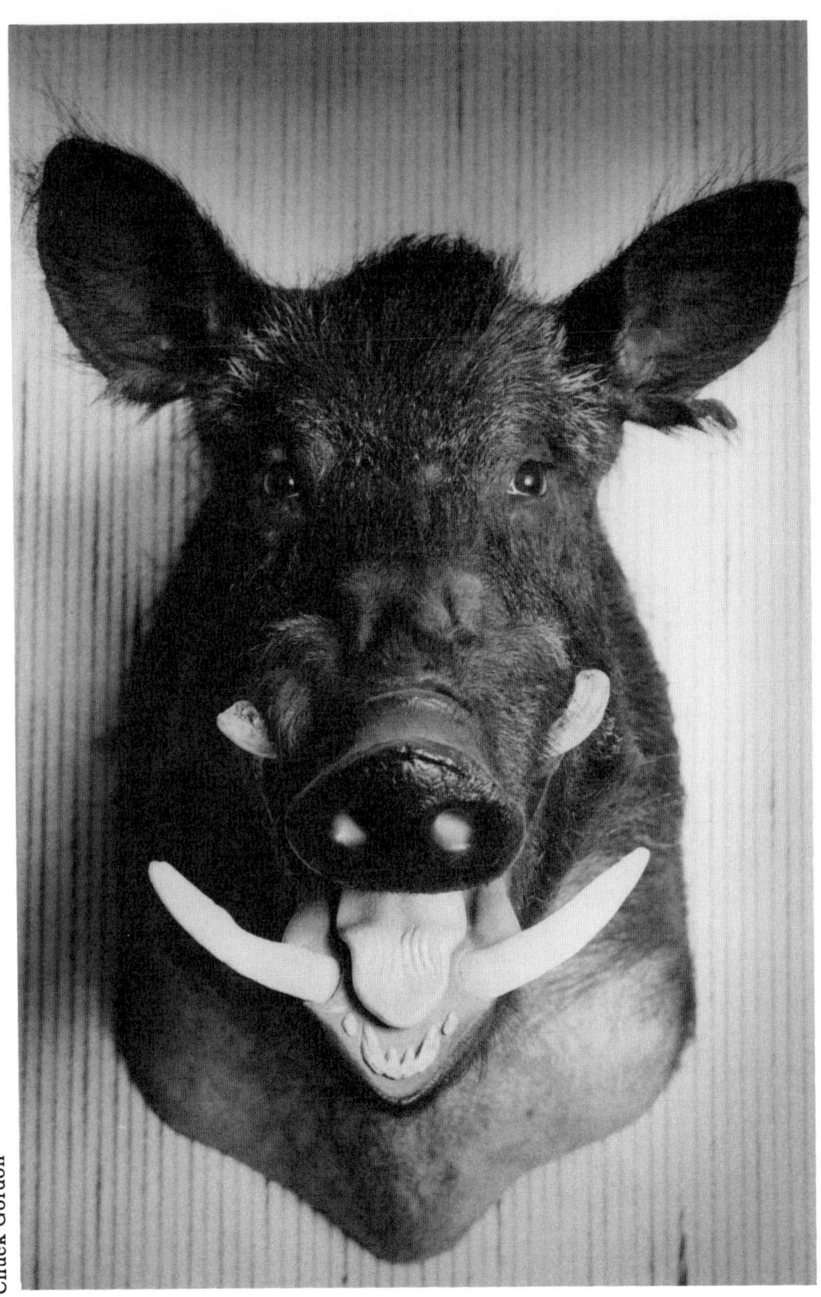

Chuck Gordon

Russian Boar

Chuck Gordon

Extremely heavy horned Blackbuck Antelope.

Chuck Gordon

Whitetail deer. Who said Texas whitetails are the size of dogs?

Chuck Gordon

White Fallow and Spotted Fallow.

Rio Grande Turkey taken by Mike Micallef (age 7)

L. C. Klenk

Big Al prepared for a day hunting in the bush. (Notice the bush!)

CONCLUSION

Hunting with Big Al

by Wayne A. Robinson

Big Al calls the night before our exotic big game hunt and stresses the importance of an early start. No problem, I say. I'll be ready and waiting at 2:00 a.m.

1:00 AM — Alarm clock rings. I can't believe it. I reach over and punch the button and lie back down to rest my eyes for just a second.

2:30 AM — Hear horn honking, and someone banging on the door, yelling and ringing the doorbell. It's Big Al. He's pissed. I explain what's happened. He doesn't understand and keeps muttering about calling me the night before for nothing.

My plan, to get up early enough to pack before he arrives, is in trouble. Big Al volunteers to help without my asking. We throw everything except the kitchen sink into the pickup.

3:00 AM — We hit the highway and head south. Big Al starts calming down. He asks which gun I brought.

3:15 AM — Drive back home to pick up gun. Big Al doesn't handle stress very well.

3:30 AM — Big Al asks to drive. He starts driving too fast. Officer doesn't understand. Big Al just sits staring.

4:00 AM — Set up camp. Forgot my tent. Big Al's eyes start watering.

4:30 AM — We head for the woods. Big Al wants to hunt alone.

6:05 AM — I see eight axis deer.

6:06 AM — Take aim and squeeze trigger.

6:07 AM — CLICK.

6:08 AM — Load gun while watching deer go over the hill.

8:00 AM — Head back to camp.

9:00 AM — Still looking for camp.

10:00 AM — Realize I don't know where camp is.

NOON — Fire gun for help.

12:05 PM — So hungry, I snack on wild berries.

12:10 PM — Fire gun again. Several times. Run out of bullets.

12:15 PM — Eight axis come back.

12:20 PM — Strange feeling in stomach.

12:30 PM — Realize I must have eaten poison berries.

12:45 PM —	Big Al finds me.
12:55 PM —	Rushes me to hospital to have stomach pumped.
3:00 PM —	Arrive back at camp. Big Al not saying much.
3:30 PM —	Feeling good again and leave camp to find axis.
4:00 PM —	Return to camp for ammunition.
4:01 PM —	Load gun. Leave camp again.
5:00 PM —	Empty gun on squirrel that's bugging me.
6:00 PM —	Return to camp. Axis grazing in camp.
6:01 PM —	Reload gun.
6:02 PM —	Fire gun.

6:03 PM — Hit pickup.

6:05 PM — Big Al arrives dragging big axis buck.

6:06 PM — Repress desire to shoot Big Al.

6:07 PM — Kick ground and trip over log. Fall into fire.

6:10 PM — Change clothes, throw burned ones into fire. Big Al cussing a lot and talking loud.

6:15 PM — I climb in pickup and leave Big Al still cussing.

6:25 PM — Pickup boils over. Bullet hole in radiator.

6:26 PM — Start walking.

6:30 PM — Stumble and fall; gun falls in the mud.

6:35 PM — Meet bear.

6:36 PM — Take aim.

6:37 PM — Fire gun; barrel plugged with mud and explodes in face.

6:38 PM — Mess pants.

6:39 PM — Climb tree.

Two Hours and Twenty-One Minutes Later...

9:00 PM — Bear leaves. Wrap #$%&@* gun around tree.

9:15 PM — Start walking home.

10:15 PM — Police stop me; they don't believe my story.

10:45 PM — Call home; wife doesn't believe my story either.

MIDNIGHT — In jail cell; I don't believe my story.

SUNDAY — Watch football game on TV, slowly tearing up all hunting licenses into small pieces. Place them in envelope, and mail to Wildlife Department with detailed instructions on where to place them.

The reference to Tommy Thompson appearing on page 135 in this book is in error. Tommy Thompson is in no way associated with "Texotics". He is owner and operator of CENTRAL TEXAS HUNTS, Route 1, Box 52, Medina, TX 78055. See CENTRAL TEXAS HUNTS, page 222.

Dear Sportsman,

The following is a list of outfitters, guides, taxidermists, and hunting facilities, which support big game hunting in Texas.

While I have hunted and worked with a number of these companies, a successful hunting trip requires careful coordination and preparation. Each company has different skills and abilities that may or may not be suited to your particular needs. I urge each hunter to consider their individual requirements, and book with the companies that fit their own hunting style.

A. M. Micallef
President,
Clear Fork Ranch, Inc.

TAXIDERMIST

Woodbury Taxidermy, Inc.
P.O. Box 510 • 101 Junction Hwy. East
Ingram, Texas 78025

Contact:
Jimmy Dieringer: 512/367-5855 (day)
512/367-5392 (evenings & weekends)

Neal Coldwell: 512/367-5081 (day)
512/634-7207 (evenings & weekends)

Description: We specialize in big game from North America, Africa, Asia, and Europe, as well as our own Texas native and exotic game. We receive trophies continuously from Alaska, Canada, and various countries overseas, that keep us in contact with many of the major outfitters. When your trophies arrive at Woodbury Taxidermy, they will receive the special attention they deserve, a lifetime leather tan, and the precision artwork and taxidermy that will restore each trophy to its original state.

Hunting Season: At Woodbury Taxidermy, hunting season lasts all year long. However, during the Texas Whitetail Season, we are open seven days a week and can be reached 24 hours a day at various telephone numbers listed outside our showroom. Please feel free to call or write for a free price list and brochure.

Y.O. Ranch®

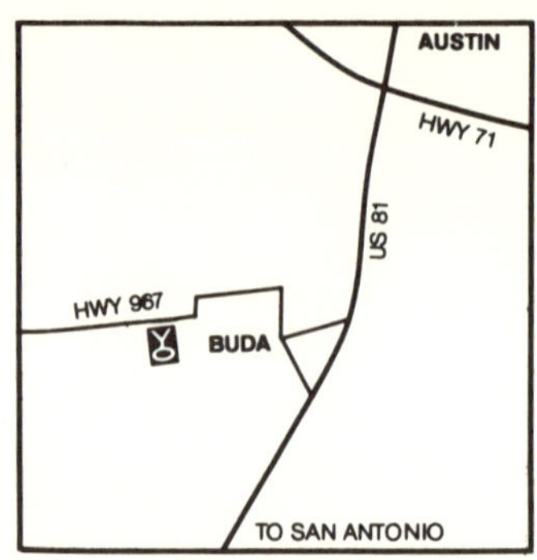

Y.O. Ranch Onion Creek Lodge
P.O. Box 957
Buda, Texas 78610
512/295-3953

Description: This 5,000 acre ranch offers some of the world's finest hunting for Axis, Blackbuck, and Bobwhite Quail.

Location: Thirty miles south of Austin on highway 967. (See map).

Available Game: Axis, Blackbuck Antelope, Whitetail Deer, Dove and Quail.

Hunting Season: Exotics hunted year-round. Whitetail Deer, Dove and Quail are controlled by state seasons.

Accomodations: All meals are provided. The lodge can accomodate twelve people with cordial lodge staff to see to your comfort.

Reservations: Contact Bo Wafford.

The atmosphere is friendly and relaxing, with home-cooked meals. This was a favorite retreat of Lyndon B. Johnson.

Y.O. Ranch®

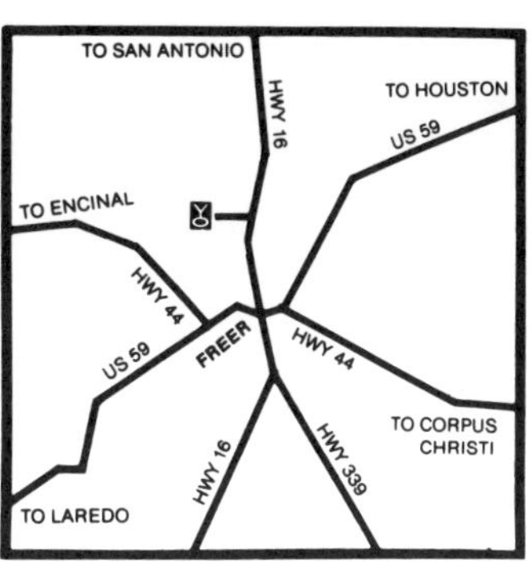

Y.O. Tomas Ranch
P.O. Box 563
Freer, Texas 78357
512/640-3222

Description: 44,000 acre ranch offers the chance of harvesting some of the best Whitetail Deer in the world. Low rolling brush country with a few limestone ridges and teeming with wildlife.

Location: Located 111 miles south of San Antonio, in the heart of Muy Grande Whitetail country.

Available Game: Whitetail Deer, Bobcat, Coyote, Feral Hog, Javelina, Mountain Lion, Russian Boar, Bobwhite Quail, and Blue Quail.

Hunting Season: Year-round hunting, except for state controlled hunting seasons.

Accomodations: New lodge can accomodate up to 16 hunters, with home-cooked meals included.

Reservations: Contact Louis Schreiner.

Hunters from around the world often visit the Tomas Ranch because it offers superior trophies. Almost all deer hunting is done from blinds.

Y.O. Ranch®

Y.O. Ranch
Mountain Home, Texas 78058
512/640-3222

Description: 50,000 acre hunting ranch. It's the largest private hunting area of its type in the world. Stocked with game animals from all parts of the world.

Available Game: Axis, Blackbuck Antelope, Corsican Ram, Snow White Corsican Rams, Wild Spanish Goat, Black Rams, Mouflon Sheep, Sika Deer, Fallow Deer, Aoudad Sheep, Y.O. Ibex, Turkey, Whitetail Deer, Elk, Russian Boar, Beisa Oryx, Gemsbok Oryx, Scimitar-horned Oryx, and Bobcat.

Hunting Season: Year-round for all except for state controlled game.

Accomodations: First class old-restored cabins with all ameneties. Can accomodate 40 hunters overnight. Also have home-cooked meals.

Reservations: Contact Louis Schreiner.

Hunting is done Safari Style. No game-no pay policy.
Will furnish rifle if needed.

HILL RANCH

YEAR ROUND EXOTIC HUNTING

Terry Hill
106 Glendale
Del Rio, Texas 78840
512/775-6125

T. L. Hill
116 Ridgewood
Del Rio, Texas 78840
512/775-4330

Description: Small operation that breeds their own animals and stresses quality animals, as well as quality hunts. Believes in old-fashioned hunting and enjoying the fun of the hunt as much as getting a trophy animal. Have produced several gold medal trophies of each type sheep.

Available Game: Pure Mouflon Sheep, Black Hawaiian, White Texas Dall, the Unique Hill Ranch Ram, Blackbuck Antelope, and other exotics on request. Also have Texas native Whitetail Deer, Spring Turkey, and Mexican Trophy Hunts.

Hunting Season: Year-round hunting for exotics. State controlled seasons for others.

Accomodations: Rustic cabins on ranches or motels in nearby Del Rio.

Reservations: Contact Terry Hill.

Some of those that have hunted at the Hill Ranch include John Wootters of "Petersen's Hunting," M. R. James of "Bowhunter," and Cameron Hopkins of "Handgunner."

OUTFITTER GUIDE

TOMMY THOMPSON
Central Texas Hunts
Route 1, Box 52
Medina, Texas 78055
512/589-7703

Description: Outfitter-guide hunting on many different ranches which total 50,000 acres. Most of these ranches are on the Edwards Plateau.

Available Game: Axis, Fallow, Sika, Blackbuck Antelope, Mouflon Sheep, Corsican Sheep, White and Black Corsican, Aoudad, Four-horn Sheep, Russian Boar, Wild Spanish Goat, Red Deer.

Hunting Season: Year-round hunting season for exotics. Regular state-controlled hunting seasons for Whitetail Deer and turkey.

Reservations: Contact Tommy or Pam Thompson.

Accomodations: A-One Lodging and Food.

For references refer to the Burkett Trophy Game Records of Texas. We strive for trophies on all hunts!!

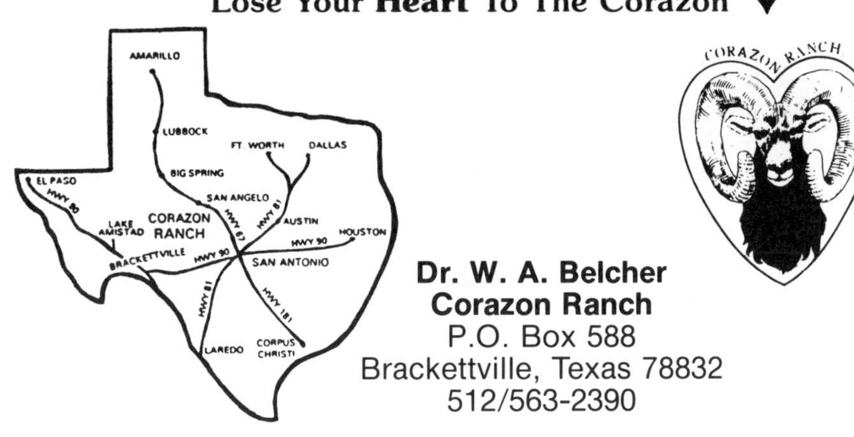

Dr. W. A. Belcher
Corazon Ranch
P.O. Box 588
Brackettville, Texas 78832
512/563-2390

Description: The Corazon is a 20 minute drive from Fort Clark. It's topography varies from rough ridges covered with semi-desert plants, to meadows of native grass and stands of oak.

Location: 125 miles west of San Antonio, 30 miles east of Del Rio, and 8 miles north of Brackettville at the end of Farm Road 2804.

Available Game: (Mid-October to Mid-March) Texas Dall, Axis, Blackbuck Antelope (when available), Corsican Ram, Catalina Goat, Mouflon Ram, Aoudad, Black Hawaiian Sheep.

(September through January) Sika Deer, Fallow, European Red Deer (when available).

Also recently included: Addax, Scimitar-horned Oryx, Formosan Sika, Dybowski Sika, Western Caucasus Tur, and Iranian Red Sheep.

(State Controlled Hunting) Whitetail Buck, Whitetail Doe, Rio Grande Turkey Gobbler, Javelina, Quail-Bob White or Blue, and Mourning Dove.

Accomodations: An inexpensive motel, eight miles from the Corazon. Fort Clark Motel offers a rare glimpse into history, combined with modern comfort. The motel has a bar and restaurant.

Reservations: For hunting reservations contact Corazon Ranch. For lodging, contact Fort Clark Motel: 512/563-2493.

Our Exotic hunts are guaranteed!!

Route 1, Box 60
Bandera, Texas 78003

Description: The Flying "A" Ranch covers almost 11,000 acres with 6500 acres devoted to Exotics. The ranch is located in the beautiful Hill Country.

Available Game: Axis, Blackbuck Antelope, Fallow, Sika Manchurian, Red Stag European, Rams Corsican, Mouflon and Texas Dall, Aoudad, Persian Ibex, Whitetail Deer and Turkey.

Hunting Season: Whitetail Deer and Turkey: November to January. Axis, Blackbuck Antelope, Rams and Aoudad: year round. Fallow, Manuchurian Sika, and Red Stag European: October to March 15.

Accomodations: Bandera Inn, Flying L Ranch.

Reservations: Contact Emmit E. Schmidt, Sr., Flying "A" Ranch, Rt. 1, Box 60, Bandera, TX 78003. Phone: 512/796-4750.

Our policy is no kill-no pay. That means there is no other charge than that of the hunt.

My Hunting Journal

Date ______________________ Time ____________________

State/Province/Country ____________________________

Hunting Areas/Camps ______________________________

Hunting Companions _______________________________

Outfitter _______________________________________

Guide ____

Address ____

____

Gun Used ____

Trophy Taken _____________________________ Score ________

Date Entered in Record Book ______________________________

"THE HUNT":

____

____

____

____

____

____

____

____

____

____

____

____

____

____

Date ______________________ Time ____________________

State/Province/Country ______________________________

Hunting Areas/Camps ________________________________

Hunting Companions _________________________________

Outfitter _______________________________________

Guide ____

Address ____

____

Gun Used ____

Trophy Taken ____________________________________ Score ________

Date Entered in Record Book _________________________________

"THE HUNT":

____

____

____

____

____

____

____

____

____

____

____

____

____

____

Date ____________ Time ____________

State/Province/Country ____________

Hunting Areas/Camps ____________

Hunting Companions ____________

Outfitter ____________

Guide ____________

Address ____________

____

Gun Used ____________

Trophy Taken ____________ Score ____________

Date Entered in Record Book ____________

"THE HUNT":

Date ______________________ Time ______________________

State/Province/Country ______________________

Hunting Areas/Camps ______________________

Hunting Companions ______________________

Outfitter ______________________

Guide ______________________

Address ______________________

____

Gun Used ______________________

Trophy Taken ______________________ Score __________

Date Entered in Record Book ______________________

"THE HUNT":

____

____

____

____

____

____

____

____

____

____

____

____

____

____

Date ______________________ Time ____________________

State/Province/Country ____________________________

Hunting Areas/Camps ______________________________

Hunting Companions _______________________________

Outfitter _______________________________________

Guide ____

Address ____

____

Gun Used ____

Trophy Taken ____ Score _________

Date Entered in Record Book _______________________________________

"THE HUNT":

____

____

____

____

____

____

____

____

____

____

____

____

____

____

Date ____________ Time ____________

State/Province/Country ____________

Hunting Areas/Camps ____________

Hunting Companions ____________

Outfitter ____________

Guide ____________

Address ____________

____

Gun Used ____________

Trophy Taken ____________ Score ____________

Date Entered in Record Book ____________

"THE HUNT":

Date ____________ Time ____________

State/Province/Country ____________

Hunting Areas/Camps ____________

Hunting Companions ____________

Outfitter ____________

Guide ____________

Address ____________

____

Gun Used ____________

Trophy Taken ____________ Score ____________

Date Entered in Record Book ____________

"THE HUNT":

____

____

____

____

____

____

____

____

____

____

____

____

____

____

Date ____________________ Time ____________________

State/Province/Country ____________________

Hunting Areas/Camps ____________________

Hunting Companions ____________________

Outfitter ____________________

Guide ____________________

Address ____________________

____

Gun Used ____________________

Trophy Taken ____________________ Score __________

Date Entered in Record Book ____________________

"THE HUNT":

____

____

____

____

____

____

____

____

____

____

____

____

____

____

Date ______________ Time ______________

State/Province/Country ______________

Hunting Areas/Camps ______________

Hunting Companions ______________

Outfitter ______________

Guide ______________

Address ______________

____

Gun Used ______________

Trophy Taken ______________ Score ______________

Date Entered in Record Book ______________

"THE HUNT":

____

____

____

____

____

____

____

____

____

____

____

____

____

____

Date ____________________ Time ____________________

State/Province/Country ____________________

Hunting Areas/Camps ____________________

Hunting Companions ____________________

Outfitter ____________________

Guide ____________________

Address ____________________

____

Gun Used ____________________

Trophy Taken ____________________ Score ________

Date Entered in Record Book ____________________

"THE HUNT":

____

____

____

____

____

____

____

____

____

____

____

____

____

____

Date ______________________ Time ____________________

State/Province/Country ____________________

Hunting Areas/Camps ____________________

Hunting Companions ____________________

Outfitter ____________________

Guide ____________________

Address ____________________

____

Gun Used ____________________

Trophy Taken ____________________ Score ________

Date Entered in Record Book ____________________

"THE HUNT":

____

____

____

____

____

____

____

____

____

____

____

____

____

____

Date ______________________ Time ____________________

State/Province/Country ____________________________

Hunting Areas/Camps ______________________________

Hunting Companions _______________________________

Outfitter ____

Guide ____

Address ____

____

Gun Used ____

Trophy Taken ____ Score ________

Date Entered in Record Book ______________________________________

"THE HUNT":

____

____

____

____

____

____

____

____

____

____

____

____

____

____

Date ____________________ Time ____________________

State/Province/Country ____________________

Hunting Areas/Camps ____________________

Hunting Companions ____________________

Outfitter ____________________

Guide ____________________

Address ____________________

____

Gun Used ____________________

Trophy Taken ____________________ Score __________

Date Entered in Record Book ____________________

"THE HUNT":

____

____

____

____

____

____

____

____

____

____

____

____

____

____

Date ____________ Time ____________

State/Province/Country ____________

Hunting Areas/Camps ____________

Hunting Companions ____________

Outfitter ____________

Guide ____________

Address ____________

____

Gun Used ____________

Trophy Taken ____________ Score ____________

Date Entered in Record Book ____________

"THE HUNT":

Date ____________ Time ____________

State/Province/Country ____________

Hunting Areas/Camps ____________

Hunting Companions ____________

Outfitter ____________

Guide ____________

Address ____________

____

Gun Used ____________

Trophy Taken ____________ Score ____________

Date Entered in Record Book ____________

"THE HUNT":

____

____

____

____

____

____

____

____

____

____

____

____

____

____